# Pondering Life's Lessons

---

### Learning from the Past

### Robert Tebo

Pondering Life's Lessons

Copyright © 2023 by Robert Tebo

All Rights Reserved. No part of this book may be reproduced in any form or by any electronic or mechanical means including information storage and retrieval systems, without permission in writing from the author. The only exception is by a reviewer, who may quote short excerpts in a review.

Published by Hallard Press LLC. www.HallardPress.com

This is a non-fiction book. It reflects the author's present recollections of experiences over time. Some names and characteristics have been changed, some events have been compressed, and some dialogue has been recreated.

Library of Congress Control Number: 2023914024

### Publisher's Cataloging-in-Publication data

Names: Tebo, Robert, author.
Title: Pondering life's lessons : learning from yesterday / Robert Tebo.
Description: The Villages, FL: Hallard Press, 2023.
Identifiers: LCCN: 2023914024 | ISBN: 978-1-951188-98-6 (paperback) | 978-1-951188-99-3 (ebook)
Subjects: LCSH Tebo, Robert. | Conduct of life. | Self-actualization (Psychology) | BISAC BIOGRAPHY & AUTOBIOGRAPHY / Personal Memoirs | BIOGRAPHY & AUTOBIOGRAPHY / Educators
Classification: LCC HQ1206 .T66 2023 | DDC 305.4--dc23

ISBN: 978-1-962326-07-0 (hardcover)
ISBN: 978-1-951188-98-6 (paperback)
ISBN: 978-1-951188-99-3 (book)

# Contents

Introduction ix
xi

**Section One: In the Beginning**

1. How About Me? — 1
2. Do You Remember Me? — 14
3. Love at First Sight — 17
4. Our Second Child — 21
5. The Most Important Lesson of My Life — 24
6. The Marriage Rules — 29
7. Three Toasts — 33
8. Nana and TGO — 37
9. Brady and B — 39
10. Eva — 42
11. Jackson James — 45
12. Dear Kate — 47
13. March 30th — 49
14. The Hippies Are Gone — 51
15. A Father's Perspective — 55
16. Courage — 58
17. A Priceless Gift — 61
18. Trust — 63
19. The Wesco Gas Station — 67
20. Tegestology — 73
21. Time — 75

**Section Two: Family and Friends** — 77

22. 500 Chunks — 78
23. It's Gonna Rain Again — 80
24. Ma and Pa Tebo — 83
25. Margaret and Harrison — 89
26. AKA Woody — 95
27. Two Bits from My Past — 97

| | |
|---|---|
| 28. Born to Be Wild | 101 |
| 29. Have You Stayed Here Before? | 103 |
| 30. James A. Marvin | 106 |
| 31. The Patsy | 109 |
| 32. The Underachiever | 113 |
| 33. Thank You, Ken | 116 |
| 34. Jay and the Americans | 121 |
| 35. Another Poker Tale | 124 |
| 36. Like You Mean It | 127 |
| 37. Wise Beyond Her Years | 129 |
| 38. My Resourceful Father | 132 |
| 39. Learn Something New | 136 |
| 40. My Three Wise Men | 143 |
| 41. Ed at 100 | 146 |
| 42. Ed at 103 | 148 |
| 43. Ed at 105 | 150 |
| 44. If I Were You I'd | 152 |
| 45. For One Hour | 154 |
| **Section Three: My Sudden Surprise** | 159 |
| 46. The Back of the Cards | 160 |
| 47. Sorry For Your Loss | 162 |
| 48. Something More | 164 |
| 49. The Stain | 167 |
| 50. 51 Years and Sixteen Days | 169 |
| 51. 3:16 | 171 |
| 52. The Worst Thing | 173 |
| 53. My New Seating Chart | 175 |
| 54. Losers | 180 |
| 55. Anxiety | 182 |
| 56. Thank You, Obadiah | 185 |
| 57. Tears | 188 |
| 58. Spaghetti and Applesauce | 190 |
| 59. My Elephant | 192 |
| 60. Widower | 194 |
| 61. A Better Way | 197 |
| 62. $15 | 199 |

| | |
|---|---|
| 63. Life Lessons | 203 |
| 64. The Red Plate | 205 |
| About the Author | 209 |

*To Ruth, David, Elizabeth and Michael*
*Thank you for being my most important people and for helping me* ***live*** *my story. Thanks, too, for sharing yours with me. LYTTMAB*

# Introduction

I've listened to and told stories all my life. My dad was my original storyteller. He spoke from experience and recounted memories from growing up and living life. He was a simple man with simple tastes. He was honest in all his dealings, and he *loved* children.

I'm a baby boomer who grew up in the suburbs of Detroit. My mother and father both came from large families, so I had several pairs of aunts and uncles. I knew both sets of grandparents and had them in my life during my early years.

I am the oldest of three children. I had several cousins and much of my family's social life centered on family gatherings in each other's homes. We celebrated every holiday together with potlucks, picnics, and birthday cakes.

My favorite part of each of these gatherings was the evening. I was the second oldest of the group of eight cousins who gathered most often. As evening came, the younger cousins went to bed while the adults did adult things. Adult things included playing cards, drinking a beer or two, and telling stories. No TV, no cell phones, no personal devices of any kind.

The stories were remembrances of days and events they were

happy to recount and share. Most were joyful tales. There were many laughs and, I expect some exaggerations.

The best part for me was to be able to "stay up." Staying up meant I got to listen to the stories. The stories I heard were a verbal history of the events that formed our extended family. Over the years I have retold these tales and added several of my own.

As my own children have grown, I realize that a family's "story" is its legacy for future generations. This book is an attempt to retell these stories so that others may share a laugh, gain some insight, and discover that each of us, and our experiences, should be celebrated. While I expect most entries will be associated with my seventy plus years, I hope to share some insight through the stories I recall from "staying up."

# Section One

## In the Beginning

## Chapter 1

## How About Me?

I met my wife, Ruth, in the fall of 1969. We were both first year teachers at Plainwell Junior High in Plainwell, Michigan. I didn't like her when we first met. I thought that she was too brash for a first-year teacher.

There were five newbies at the junior high that year: Ruth, Dave, Rick, Dorothy, and me. Tony was new to the staff too but had taught there in the past. Grandville was the new band instructor but had been the high school principal the year before.

Ruth walked around like she owned the place. That was too much for me. I found out a few days after our first meeting that she had graduated from Plainwell and had most of the staff as teachers herself just a few years prior. My first cool impression of her began to thaw after this revelation.

Ruth and I went on our first official date on Valentine's Day in 1970. It was a staff party for junior high and the beginning of our relationship. We were both dating others and exclusivity was not in the cards for several months. We saw more and more of each other but there were always others in the mix. I believe her mix was larger than mine. There was one girl other than Ruth whom I dated the most, but others dropped in from time to time.

Sometime in late 1970 or early 1971, Ruth started talking about marriage (at least that's the way I remember it). I was not in that place and so the talk led nowhere. I was narrowing my focus to her, but I wasn't ready to "tie the knot."

In the spring of 1971, we both bought new cars. I traded my 1967 Mustang convertible for a 1971 Ford Torino. (One of the biggest mistakes of my life.) Ruth traded her 1963 Volkswagen for a 1971 Ford Pinto. While we both bought Ford products, we bought them from different dealers. The new car purchases brought about a series of changes that altered both our lives forever.

Ruth bought her car from Mike who was interested in Ruth for more than just selling a car. They started dating, we stopped, and they became engaged during that summer.

After returning to work in the fall of 1971, I stopped into Ruth's room on Friday after school. Several students from the prior school year had returned from high school to visit Ruth too. The students, Ruth, and I shared a lot of stories. Ready to move on for the weekend, I told Ruth that I planned to make a stop on the way home. Ruth said that she might make the same stop. We had both tired of the conversation with the students and this was a way to move on. The stop was the Hi-Lo, a small neighborhood bar. We had stopped on other Friday afternoons over the past couple of years but always with other teachers looking to wind down from the week's work. This was the first Friday of our third year of teaching and my final Friday as a single man.

Our stop at the Hi-Lo was eventful. We were more engrossed in the conversation than the drinking or the sparse afternoon crowd. We continued our reminiscence that began at the school with the students, and Ruth reviewed the details of her sister's wedding the month before. I knew her sister, Kathy, and her new husband, Tim. The wedding review and continued conversation lead to tears. From Ruth – not me. She ran off to the bathroom to compose herself.

When she returned, so did the tears. When I asked her why she was crying she said, "I don't want to marry Mike."

Looking back, my reply to this statement could have taken several different turns. I could have said, "Why not?" or "That's too bad." or "I never thought that you should marry a car salesman whose greatest claim to fame was selling a garbage truck for a large commission."

But I didn't. As quickly as she had said, "I don't want to marry Mike." I fired back, "How about me?" The tears stopped instantly.

My proposal wasn't very flashy, but it was sincere. I hadn't rehearsed it, but I had given it some thought. Not at that moment but over the time we weren't together. I had passed on the opportunity several months prior by "not being ready," so this time was more like, "Ready or not, here I come."

I don't remember Ruth's exact words, but her reply sounded something like, "When?" Followed by my, "I don't care when. Whenever you want." Then Ruth's, "Well if we are going to do this, let's do it right away." The conversation moved along very quickly. I think our decision to seize the moment ensured we'd follow through. Mike was Ruth's third engagement. I had been engaged once myself. We weren't good at being engaged.

We left the Hi-Lo with no concrete plan other than to figure out how we could get married as soon as possible. We took my car and left hers behind. As we drove, we talked. We were going to find out how, when, and where we could elope. It wasn't an elaborate plan, but it was deliberate. Funny what details you remember at a time like this. I remember very clearly that she was wearing a collared t-shirt dress with lime green, navy blue, and white stripes. And it was short.

We drove first to my apartment in Kalamazoo. During the drive Ruth remembered an old, family friend. Perhaps Judge Westra could marry us or at least point us in the right direction. Ruth called him. While sympathetic to our cause, the judge wasn't much help. I had heard, or thought I'd heard, that you could get married in Indiana without a blood test. Turns out that rumor was incorrect.

I also heard that Las Vegas was a possibility. I picked up the phone, called the telephone operator in Las Vegas, Nevada and asked her if couples who came to Las Vegas could be married immediately or if there was a waiting period. Two surprising things happened during that conversation. 1. You could actually speak to a real person, on the phone, long distance without a charge, and 2. You could get married, immediately, no waiting, no blood test, just show up and say, "I do."

Decision made. We were going to Vegas. Chicago was the closest major city to Kalamazoo, so I called the airport to see when we could catch a plane. I booked a flight on the first plane out in the morning. We paid for the round-trip tickets by charging $400.00 to Ruth's new credit card.

I packed a bag and discovered I had no clean slacks to wear to my wedding. We'd have to stop to buy a pair. My sports coat and suit were at the cleaners, so I borrowed a blue blazer (without asking) from my friend, Mike. On the way out of the building we ran into my roommate, Chuck. Chuck was surprised to see Ruth. She'd been absent from our lives for several months. When he asked what we were doing, the reply was simple, "We're on our way to get married." He didn't believe us at first, but disbelief turned to excitement and then laughter. We waved, and he chuckled as we walked down the hall.

We drove from my apartment to Ruth's. We arrived about ten minutes later and thirty seconds prior to her about-to-be former fiancé, Mike. They had a date that evening that she had forgotten to mention. The date, and I expect his heart, were about to be broken.

Ruth and I arrived a split second before Mike and were walking towards her apartment when his car pulled in. That's when I learned of their scheduled six o'clock date. That was a surprise for me. Of the two surprises Mike and I received within a minute of each other, I'll go with mine. While I learned of their date, he was about to be given the old "heave ho."

The next portion of this recounting of this milestone in my life is based upon what "I think" happened because I wasn't there for every single moment.

(Fact) Ruth walked towards his car and got in. (Conjecture) Once inside the car Mike said something like… "Ruth, is that Bob? He's a lot better looking than I remember. Taller too."

Truth be told, they broke up sitting in his green 1971 Mustang. He wasn't happy and didn't take the news well. The only thing that I know for sure is he wanted his engagement ring returned, and she had to dig it out of her purse.

She got out of the car, walked towards me, and he drove away. (When the movie comes out, this will be shown on a split screen with no dialog, just dramatic music.)

We walked into her apartment and Ruth started packing. The packing was moving forward nicely when there was a knock on the door. (Suspenseful pause)

It was Chuck. He'd reported our impending nuptials to two of our former apartment neighbors, Jean and Debbie. The five of us held an excited conversation while Ruth packed. "This is so exciting!" "I've never known anyone who actually eloped before!" and "Are you really going to do this?" Followed by, "Yes, we are!"

We needed to add new underwear to our shopping list because Ruth was clean out. (Pun intended) We asked Chuck and the girls to retrieve Ruth's car from the Hi-Lo parking lot and then we headed to Steketee's Department Store for our shopping needs. We ran into the parents of a high school friend of Ruth's, Mr. and Mrs. Labby, in the underwear department. We shared our news with them and they, in turn, told us that they had eloped. Small world. The first married couple we encounter is fellow elopers. (Probably not a word)

After we completed our shopping, we headed to Chicago. As we crossed the Illinois line, seven people knew of our impending elopement: Chuck, Jean, Debbie, the Labbys, Judge Westra, and Mike.

The drive is completely gone from my memory. We drove, and I know we spoke, but I remember zip, zero, nada. We checked into a hotel at about ten that night.

We checked out in the morning, completed our drive to the airport, parked my car, and boarded our plane. Boring but truthful.

We landed in Las Vegas, rented a car, and drove down the Las Vegas strip. The drive took us by big name casinos with what we expected to hold upscale, high-priced hotel rooms – Hacienda, Tropicana, Aladdin, The Dunes, MGM, Caesars Palace, Flamingo Hilton, The Desert Inn, Silver Slipper, Castaways, Frontier, Stardust, Sands, Riviera, Sahara, Circus Circus, the Thunderbird, and dozens of walk-in-and-get-married chapels.

Ruth didn't want to get married in a little chapel on the strip even if it had a pretty name like Little Chapel of the Silver Bells or Chapel of the Flowers. She started to cry.

We needed a place to stay and a place to get married. Two equally important objectives. I told her we would explore our marriage options and avoid the million plus chapels. (If you were married in one of these chapels, I hope things are going well for you. It just wasn't in the cards for us.)

We located the Tod Motor Hotel on the north end of the strip past the major casinos and booked a room at $25.00 for the night. Once inside the room, I started to make phone calls to locate a site to get married. I was raised Catholic so it only made sense that I would contact a Catholic church for guidance. The yellow pages had a listing for a church in Boulder City. Boulder City sounded friendlier than Las Vegas, so I called it. I ended up speaking to Father Boulder (really) and asked if he could marry us. I explained that I was Catholic, but my intended was Baptist. His reply was direct and politically insensitive.

"You haven't got a Chinaman's chance" and he spoke it with an Irish brogue. No church wedding for us.

My second call was more helpful. I called one of the "I don't want to get married in one of those" chapels. They wanted to know where I was so they could send a limo "right away." They would supply a wedding dress, a tux, flowers, photos, a cake, the works. I could select from a multitude of services or opt for a pay-one-price option. They wanted to be as helpful as I would allow them. I just wanted to know where to obtain a marriage license. "The Clark County Courthouse" was the reply. "Tell us where you are, and we'll be right over." I provided a quick "No, thanks" and hung up.

We dressed for the ceremony. Ruth wore a short blue dress with little turtles (kind of a seaside look). I wore the borrowed blue blazer and my new maroon, polyester dress slacks (what a stud). We got directions from the front desk and made the quick trip to the courthouse.

We weren't the only ones intent on getting married that day. The court bailiff directed us to a line of people looking for the same "how do you get a marriage license" information. We saw people in wedding dresses and tuxes (over kill), mink stoles (prior to PETA) and guys with rolled-up white tee-shirt sleeves (at least the shirt *had* sleeves). Then, there was us, the all-American cover of Look and Life magazine, model prospects. We were beautiful.

The line progressed quickly. As the clerk processed our license, she told us we could get married by a Justice of the Peace in the courthouse. We approached the bailiff that had helped us earlier for additional directions. Without any words being exchanged, he pointed upstairs.

We found the Justice of the Peace office with a sign stating a ceremony was in progress. We sat down and waited for about three minutes. As the happy couple left, we were invited into the office. The Justice welcomed us and asked if we had attendees. "No" was our simple reply. "No problem," came from the justice, followed by "Do you have a ring?" Turns out we did. Ruth was wearing a pearl ring her dad had given her. "That will work just fine." Ruth handed him the ring and the ceremony began.

I don't recall much about the office. There were some artificial plants and a picture or two. I do remember very clearly that it was just the three of us in the room. As the justice started the ceremony,

Ruth began to cry. I laughed. Here we were on the most important day of our life crying, laughing, "repeating after me," and then, "I doing." Five minutes later, I could "kiss the bride" and we were married.

Later, when I examined our marriage license, it had been signed by the bailiff, the marriage license clerk (our witnesses who were not in the room), and the Justice. The entire bill came to $15.00. Pretty simple process.

As we exited the courthouse, we saw a clock and a thermometer. It was 1:00 p.m. PST, 101 degrees, Saturday, September 11, 1971.

On our way back to "The Tod" we stopped at a party store. We bought a package of Twinkies and a bottle of champagne. We made a toast to ourselves, ate our "wedding cake" and changed our clothes. Then we called Ruth's parents.

Ruth's mom answered the phone. There was no small talk. I was listening to one end of the conversation that went something like this. "Hello, Mom. I'm calling from Las Vegas to tell you and dad that I got married." Kate, Ruth's mom, must have asked 'to whom' because the next thing that I heard from Ruth was "Bob."

Now that tells you something. Ruth is engaged to Mike, calls her mom to tell her that she'd eloped, and mom asked who she married. She didn't even provide a check list. It was an opened ended "Who can it be?" kind of question.

Ruth started to speak, but the tears won out again, and I took the phone. I said all the things that a guy should say. "I love her." "I'll take good care of her." "You can count on me." And I meant every word. We closed the conversation with, "We'll see you tomorrow."

After the phone call, we got in the car and drove to Hoover Dam. We bought a camera, took turns taking each other's picture at the dam (way before selfies) and then took a tour. Our trip was life-changing, educational, and a possible tax deduction.

The next morning, we had the champagne brunch at The Sahara. We were celebrating and planning for our "what's next" when the tears returned. How many times can one girl cry? My only thought was Ruth was starting to regret the whole "How about me?" question and reply. I offered up a possible solution. "If you're having second thoughts, we can get a divorce, right now, and no one will know the difference. We can get a divorce in the same amount of time as it took us to get married. We can tell everyone that we changed our minds."

That was the perfect thing to say. While the tears didn't subside, she did know my intentions were sincere. I did love her. I did want her to be happy. And I did want her to stop crying.

A few sniffles later we were on a plane headed back to Chicago.

It was early evening when we landed and I called our new building principal, Burton Cave, to tell him that I would need a sub for my classroom the next day. "You need to get one for Ruth VanBruggen too. We eloped over the weekend."

"Sure, you did. Is she going to drive a truck with you too?"

Funny thing. About three weeks before school started that fall, several of the male members of the junior high teaching staff decided it would be a good idea for me to call Burton to play a joke on him. While we all planned the joke, I did the talking. I told him I had driven a truck all summer and that I liked my new job. I was going to quit teaching and become a teamster. He bought the story before he heard everyone laughing in the background, and he wasn't going to fall for another one of my "jokes."

"No, really," I pleaded. "I'm telling the truth. We both need subs. We'll be in later in the morning to explain." I leaned out of the phone booth so he could hear the announcement "Flight 702 to Tokyo, Japan is now boarding." He heard it, laughed, and said, "Ok, I'll see the two of you tomorrow."

We drove back to Kalamazoo and spent the night with Chuck at our apartment. The next morning, we drove to Ruth's mom and dad's house in Plainwell. Her dad was working, but we spoke with her mom and that conversation was the key to dry eyes. We recounted the weekend's events, and once again, I committed myself to taking care of Ruth.

After speaking with her mom, Ruth and I drove over to the junior high. The place exploded. Burton couldn't keep a secret. "They're here! They're here!" rang out from students hanging out from the classroom windows. As we walked up the stairs towards Burton's office, kids rushed out to see us and talk, teachers shook our hands, and more than one welled up with tears. We were about to become the biggest story that town had shared in years.

We met briefly with Burton who gave me $8.00 from petty cash so we could "have lunch." It was decided that we would return to work on Thursday. We each visited our classroom, stopped along the way to meet with others, and were preparing to return to Ruth's parents to see her dad when we discovered that my car had been decorated while we were inside making the rounds. There was toilet paper wrapped inside and out, and rice everywhere. It was a fun mess from a bunch of people who loved us. Students filled the school's front lawn, and cheers rang out again as we "unwrapped" the car.

We drove back to Ruth's parent's house to vacuum out the rice and meet with her dad. There were a few tears from Ruth and Kate, but all in all, that meeting went well. Lou, Ruth's dad, was going to be okay with all of this. That was a huge relief to me. While we were there, Ruth called her sisters, Kathy and Shirley, so they were in the loop with all that had taken place.

My sister, Sharron, was student teaching in Grand Rapids about a half-hour from Plainwell. I wanted to tell her the news in person, so we drove up to her school. She was in an after-school staff meeting and I had her called out so we could speak with her. We briefly recounted the week-end's events and then started off on our drive to Royal Oak to break the news to my parents.

My dad was washing dishes when we walked in the side door into the kitchen. He turned around and asked what we were doing home. I told him we came to tell them we had eloped. His reply still rings clearly in our ears, "What the hell did you do that for?" and he turned to complete the dishes. My mom came down the hall and was a bit more subtle and excited. Both were obviously surprised. Heck, so were Ruth and I.

Mom called my Aunt Ruth and Uncle Harry and my Aunt Phillis and Uncle Harry. (Yes, I had two Uncle Harrys.) I called my college roommate, Gary, and his wife, Susan. Everyone came over and we recounted the events again and again as each couple arrived. My youngest sister, Jackie, joined us after her shift at Baskin-Robbins. Surprise!

The most unusual part of the trip to Royal Oak was my mom and dad giving up their double bed to the newlyweds. Awkward.

That's how the long weekend went. What we didn't know at the time was several people were circling the month of May 1972 on their calendars.

On Tuesday morning, we returned to Kalamazoo. We went to a jewelry store and purchased two gold wedding bands. Mine cost $40.00 and I expect Ruth's was about the same. (Another example of memory moments stored deeply in our brains.)

Ruth and I had a housing dilemma. Both of us had recently signed six-month apartment leases. Problem solved. One of my friends, Mike, (my friend, not Ruth's) would take over my lease. Ruth and I lived with Chuck, and upon occasion, Mike, for the remainder of the fall. We were three and/or four peas in a pod. We would pay Ruth's apartment mate, Chris, three month's rent or until she could find a new roommate. (We paid the rent for the entire three months.)

I owned a two-unit rental income property in Kalamazoo and one of the units was about to be vacated. We would move into this as soon as it became available which was scheduled to be in late October. We moved in with Ruth's parents and had her old bedroom on the second story of their remodeled farmhouse. It wasn't ideal, but nothing about the beginning of our rekindled relationship was ideal. Ruth's parents opened their home willingly and we ended up living with them for some time between three weeks and eternity.

Both our sets of parents threw parties for us. They were very nice but with major differences. The VanBruggens held a coffee and cake reception in their home on a Sunday afternoon. My mom, dad and two sisters were on hand. Ruth's two sisters, their husbands, and our two nieces were there as well. (Yes, I became an instant uncle when I said, "I do.")

The remainder of the visitors to the "open house" were fellow teachers, members of the VanBruggen's church, assorted neighbors, and a variety of business associates. We received a boat load of gifts. Luckily, we had "registered" just like normal people who are about to get married (silver, china, crystal, the works), but we did so after the fact. We opened each gift at an appropriate gift-opening time after most of the people arrived and the cake was cut. There were several envious ladies in the crowd while most of the guys stuck with conversing and eating cake.

The Tebo approach to an after-the-fact party looked like I expect that it would have looked if it had happened under a normal timeline. My parents rented a hall, provided a buffet dinner, an open bar, and a band. Did I say PARTY!!! It's the first, last, and only time (FLO) that I saw my father-in-law have a drink. Lou and Kate may have actually danced. (Another FLO)

Ruth and I spent the night in a hotel room and opened "our envelopes." We received $600 in cash which was exactly $600 more in cash than we received at the VanBruggen open house. I point out this difference to make an observation. In 1971, open houses on the west side of the state were nicely appointed gatherings. Receptions in the Detroit area were more active "parties" and gifts focused on cash. We appreciated both because neither was required nor expected. (Interesting fact- we used $300 to purchase a couch that we still own and use. It's a great place to take a nap.)

The month of May 1972 came and went without any "surprises." We learned years later that some thought we "had" to get married. We didn't. We chose to get married, and so far, so good.

September 11, 1971 is the most important date in my life. March

30, 1975 (David Anthony), March 10, 1977 (Elizabeth Kathryn) and July 10, 1978 (Michael Robert) follow closely behind.

And why tell this tale, you may ask.

The special moments in our lives should be remembered and shared. Three amazing new kids (Lindsay, Kate, and Sutton) and three wonderful grandchildren (Brady, Eva, and young Jackson James) have joined our family during the past several years. We want all of them to know the story through our eyes.

Over the years we have recounted the truths of our brief engagement and marriage in Las Vegas to hundreds of people. Most have found it interesting and unusual.

I have been encouraged to "write the story down." I waited a long time. Better late than never.

And so, it is written.

## Chapter 2

## Do You Remember Me?

Ruth and I took a three-week, belated honeymoon, during the summer of 1972. One of our stops on our southern swing was Biloxi, Mississippi. I have two memories of that stop. First, there were the cockroaches that Ruth discovered in our motel room when she switched on the bathroom light. Second, beautiful plantation style mansions lined the gulf coast between Biloxi and Gulfport. I had never seen anything like them. Our next visit took place on January 1, 1997, and our third in the summer of 2004. The mansions were just as beautiful each time we visited.

We've returned to Biloxi since then but each of those visits has been post-Katrina and post-beautiful plantation style mansions. Katrina took them all.

We recently traveled to Biloxi with our great friends, Jim and Diane. The first morning of our trip, a woman walked up to our breakfast table and asked, "Do you remember me?" I did. I looked into her eyes and replied, "Stacey?" That's where I first look when people ask if I remember them. People change as they age. Some get fatter, turn grey haired, develop wrinkles (that's my trifecta) but most eyes remain the same, so it's always eyes-first for me.

Stacey was a bus driver for me when I was superintendent in Britton-Macon. I haven't seen her in more than a dozen years. I have stories about Stacey that I could share, but her only real request of me was to be remembered. I do.

I was having lunch a few months ago in a favorite restaurant when a lady came up to my table and said, "Bob, it's Gracia. Remember me?" I remembered. I remember her son, John, too. When I was the elementary school principal in Addison, John and I were tight. John and I had a conversation, or two, almost every day. Gracia and I spoke briefly about our many talks during John's elementary school career. She shared and we celebrated the fact that John is a long-distance truck driver and doing very well.

After she left the table, I reminded Ruth that Gracia and her husband, Dick, left a bottle of Jim Beam in a brown paper bag on my desk for four continuous years. It came the final day of school with a note that said, "You earned this. Thank you, Gracia, Dick, and John."

Ruth and I have our mail forwarded to Florida each winter. About ten days prior to my return to Michigan, I have the post office hold my mail so I have minimal interruption to the bill paying process. When I arrive in Michigan, I go to the post office to pick up the mountain they've collected on my behalf.

Last April, a man and his wife joined me in the post office lobby when I picked up the mail. He said, "Mr. Tebo, do you remember me?"

"Yes, Scott, I remember you." His tattoos threw me off, but I remembered his eyes.

Scott was one of my elementary school students. He's 43 or 44 now. When Scott was 12, he was a member of the "Tigers" baseball team. Not the Detroit Tigers, but the Tigers I coached in the local little league program. He and another eleven players made up the roster of one of the baddest (when I say bad, I mean good) group of young hombres to ever grace the baseball fields of Addison, Michigan. We beat everyone and were the Addison Little League

Champions. To hear Scott tell the tale to his wife, we could have been world champions. He was very proud to relive the story of what he and his teammates had accomplished. He wasn't the best player on our team, but I expect that he may remember better than most. He was proud of that accomplishment and wished to share it with someone he loved even if it occurred over thirty years prior.

One of my greatest moments of pride occurred during the end of my tenure as superintendent of Britton-Macon. My last six months and David's first six months of becoming the superintendent in Michigan Center overlapped. We were the only father/son duo in the state. One day, the two of us were walking together in a local home supply store when a voice from the rear yelled out, "Hey, Mr. Tebo."

We both turned around and I quickly ran through my storehouse of eyes so I could determine the identity of this young person. The boy walked up to David and asked, "What are you doing here, Mr. Tebo?"

"Shopping with my dad." Was his simple reply.

David and my roles were reversing in the public eye. That was the moment that David stopped being "my son," and I became "his dad."

Whether your name is Stacey, Gracia, Scott, Bob, or even Biloxi, we all want to be remembered. For most of us being remembered means that we have had purpose. That while we are here, we've made a difference. We want someone to remember and share our story. And if we're still around to take part in the sharing, that makes every shared moment even better.

## Chapter 3

## Love at First Sight

The first people I loved were my parents. I believe that's probably true of most people. Over time I learned to love my two sisters, as much as a pain in the rear that I found them. It may have been automatic, but I don't remember it that way. I expect that's the path of most brothers and sisters.

As I got older, I fell in and out of love a few times. I had several girlfriends until I found the girl I chose to marry. All of those relationships began with an attraction that grew over time. I never experienced "love at first sight," and though I did believe in "lust at first sight," I didn't feel that way about love.

Forty-three years ago today, March 30, 1975, that all changed. Our first child, David, was born on Easter Sunday at 10:07 p.m. The moment I saw him, I loved him.

When Ruth and I first found out that she was pregnant, we started to study and explore what we should anticipate. We knew that being a parent was serious business and we wanted to do all we could ahead of time to be prepared for the arrival of our first child. We didn't tell anyone we were "expecting" until we were several weeks along in the "expecting" process. We felt it best to keep to ourselves until we were "ready" to share our news. Our lives were about to change. We were happy, but unwilling to have others join us until we wanted them to.

We discussed names, living arrangements, made sure that Ruth did all the right things regarding her health, and listened to Ruth's Aunt Casey (head nurse for the delivery room at Kalamazoo's Bronson Hospital) for "birthing" advice. Fathers taking part and witnessing births was a relatively new concept that became the norm in the 70's.

Ruth and I attended "expectant parent" classes. We practiced breathing techniques (slow, light accelerated, variable, expulsion, cleansing), learned physical positions to assist with the birth, and what to expect throughout the delivery. We discussed breast vs. bottle feeding. We learned the pros and cons of cloth diapers vs disposable, the various types of formulas, and the purpose of an Apgar score (appearance, pulse, grimace, activity, respiration). We knew that scores of 7, 8, and 9 were good and that 10 seldom, if ever, happens. Most importantly, we learned that when the "water breaks" we better get moving, because after all of our preparation and study (in the words of Butterfly McQueen), "we didn't know nothin' 'bout birthin' babies."

We were getting ready to drive to Plainwell to have Easter dinner with Ruth's parents when our plans changed. We drove instead to Bronson Hospital. We arrived shortly before 1:00 and our doctor joined us about an hour later. After examining Ruth, he headed back to his Easter dinner and told me that I might as well go out to eat as our baby's birth is "going to be a while." I stayed and left for my last meal as a childless man around 6:00.

When I was with Ruth, I did what I could to help her, but all of the breathing techniques and positional advice got thrown out the window when the serious contractions began. We didn't know if our child was a boy or a girl until at 10:07 the nurse announced, "It's a boy." Ruth's reply was simple and heartfelt. "My dad is going to be so happy." (Lou had three daughters and two granddaughters. He finally had a boy in his life.)

David Anthony checked in with an Apgar score of 8. The remaining numbers were: 8 pounds 5 ounces, 21 and half inches long. Ruth's diet of full packages of spinach drenched in vinegar, whole heads of lettuce with dressing each evening, and entire Bill Knapp's chocolate cakes devoured in a single session provided the nourishment that our unborn child required. She gained sixty pounds in nine months and dropped thirty-eight in one night.

That was the most important moment of my life. Everything changed. This was what "love at first sight" felt like. How can one moment change a person's life so profoundly in one split second? Forty-three years have passed yet I remember that moment like it was yesterday. It was the highest of highs.

I remained at the hospital for an hour or so, called my parents and Ruth's parents, and because of the late hour waited to call others in the morning. I couldn't sleep, my heart was pounding, my entire being was bursting with joy.

In the morning, I called everyone else I knew. While no one appeared to be as excited as me, everyone wished us well. Ruth spent several days in the hospital (you could do that back then). I spent many hours visiting her and holding our son. Ruth and David came home in a few days to our house on Reycraft Street and our life as a family began.

You can do all the planning for your family that you may like, but then life happens. Things don't always work out as planned. Perfect isn't always possible, but having a family with three children is the most important thing that I have ever done. It is my greatest accomplishment. Ruth and I raised three people who are making a difference, each in their own way. I am one proud father.

David often thanks Ruth and me for being the man that he has become and the success he enjoys. I'm proud to say that he has followed in my footsteps as a teacher, principal, and school superintendent. Truth be told, we're better people because of him and his sister and brother.

Much has changed during the last forty-three years. David has a family of his own now. Shortly after his first-born, Brady, came along he asked, "Is it possible to love someone more than you love yourself?" My reply was simple, "Yes, and now you know how I feel about you, Elizabeth, and Michael."

## Chapter 4

## Our Second Child

When Ruth and I started our family, we agreed that names were important. We wanted each of our children to have a strong name. Names that would be remembered and impactful. As teachers we were well aware that some names were designed to encourage nick names. Some names encouraged rhyming. We didn't want T names like Tommy or Tonya. Some names reminded us of former students to whom we preferred not to pay homage.

We didn't want foo-foo names like Sunshine, Rainbow, or Sky. If one of our children grew up to be president, we couldn't see them being called President Sky Tebo. Supreme Court Justice Rainbow Tebo didn't ring well either.

Our children were born in the "box of chocolates" age. We never knew what we were going to get so we had to be prepared with a name for a boy and a name for a girl. We did want to honor our family heritage but Ruth's family all came from the Netherlands, so Willaminia, Cornelia, or Ruth's father's name – Roelof – wouldn't fit the bill. Ruth didn't even want Ruth to be a choice. My side of the family had more traditional names: Margaret, Carter, Mary, and Anthony were all good strong names.

Most of all, we planned to call each of our children by their given name, so we had to enjoy saying the name. David Anthony (March 30, 1975) was our first child, Elizabeth Kathryn (March 10, 1977) our second, and Michael Robert (July 10, 1978) was third. All good names. David Anthony honored my father as well as being a first name that we both liked. Katherine and Kathryn were our mothers' names, so Elizabeth Kathryn was a good fit. By the time Michael Robert was born, I had moved on from the fact that Ruth's last fiancé was Michael and the Robert part pleased me.

Ruth and I moved to Addison, Michigan in the summer of 1977 where I was assuming the elementary school principal's position. Although I was unofficially on site and already working, I was formally hired on August 16 – the day Elvis Presley died. David was two-and-half and Elizabeth was six-months. Michael was still just a twinkle in his father's eye. Initially, I came alone and lived in three different places for each of my first three weeks: Carolyn and Roger Dixon's home (Roger was superintendent), Mary Lou and Don Dieck's home (Don was high school principal) and the Clearwater Motel (since torn down and now the site of the new home for the Adrian College rowing team). The month of September was spent in a cottage on Round Lake.

One of the highlights of our new family, and our new home, was Friday Night Football. Football in Addison was a BIG deal. That made homecoming and the homecoming parade even bigger. People like parades. My family was no different. Ruth brought David and Elizabeth to the homecoming parade. It was their first, big, public outing. This was the first time that the wife and family of the new elementary school principal were in such a large gathering and on display. Everyone had been welcoming, but this day was just a bit different. Many staff members from the various school buildings introduced themselves to Ruth. Ruth, in turn, introduced David and Elizabeth. When Kathy Bergman, a middle school teacher, was introduced to Elizabeth she said, "Oh, a little BZ." We'd never heard anyone called that before. "BZ"

Later that same weekend, Ruth and I were recounting the incident. Every time David tried to say Elizabeth, it came out Isbet. As opposed to nicknames as we were, we liked the sound of "BZ." It was unique. We thought that David would do a better job pronouncing "BZ" too. The informal name dropping by Kathy became the new official name of our very unique daughter. BZ was born. We discussed the various ways that we would spell "BZ." We were educators, and spelling was important. Beezee and BeZee were options that we discussed. But "BZ" felt, looked, and sounded just right.

I don't believe that Ruth or I thought that the name would be heard outside of our immediate family. As we started using the name on a regular basis, we never imagined that all her school friends or teachers would join us. Certainly, college would be a change. After all, even though Ruth was always Ruth, Robbie became Bob or Rob with the passing of time.

But it stuck. It stuck and it has served her well. She, like her name, is unique. She's smart, pretty, talented, a world traveler; and though she can't leap tall buildings in a single bound, she can make my heart leap that high. While I expect that most fathers believe that their daughters are the most wonderful daughters in the world, they are wrong.

# Chapter 5

# The Most Important Lesson of My Life

The most important lesson of my life was taught to me by a seven-year-old boy. He wasn't just any seven-year-old. He was mine. He turns forty a little after 1:00 p.m. today.

Michael is the third of our three children. We didn't plan to have three, but like most blessings in our life, they just happened.

Michael had a tough beginning. He was very ill and had to be hospitalized twice for a week at a time during the first few months of his life. The formula that he drank passed directly through his system, he became dehydrated, and he was very weak. Ultimately, we took him to the University of Michigan Children's Hospital where they completed a diagnosis that altered his diet and solved his problem. We nicknamed him the "Million Dollar Baby" because the new, improved formula cost about four times the amount than the one originally prescribed by our pediatrician.

Some of our friends predicted that Michael would develop on one of two paths. He would become a weak child, and have a difficult time, or he would become very strong. Their predictions were based upon their own assumptions rather than scientific fact. Those who thought he would become a strong child were correct.

I was David's, Elizabeth's, and Michael's elementary school principal. I believe all three would describe this arrangement as both a blessing and a curse. Some people treat you differently, even though it may be unintentional, when you're the "boss's" kid. I know that each one underwent some "shunning" by their peers because of me. They never complained. They just took what others doled out.

During the early eighties, the middle school principalship was added to my assignment in Addison. We promoted a teacher, Dave, to be my assistant. We were in charge of the education of over 900 students in three separate buildings. We worked together, relying on each other's strengths, to make it work.

While we traveled from building to building on the common campus, I made it a habit of being in the middle school during each lunch hour. One Wednesday, early in Michael's second grade school year, I received a phone call from one of the elementary school secretaries, Sally, letting me know that Michael was ill. Ruth was working in Adrian, so I called upon a neighbor to pick him up and care for him during the afternoon.

The following Wednesday, I received a similar call. Michael was ill. We had a clinic in the middle school. I asked Sally to have Michael walk across the elementary school playground to the middle school so I could look after him in the clinic.

A week later, on Wednesday, I received a third call from Sally. Michael was ill. "I'll be right over," I replied. I was an educator. Michael was developing a pattern of becoming ill on Wednesday during his lunch hour. I decided to stop in to meet with his teacher, Miss Perkins, a wonderful, seasoned veteran, to seek her guidance in Michael's problem.

When I walked into her room, I asked a simple question. "Miss Perkins, what happens in class after lunch on Wednesday?"

Her reply told me everything I needed to know. "We have our practice spelling test for the week. The final test is on Friday."

That was it. Spelling. Michael and I suffered from the same disease. Spellitis. (my self-diagnosed disease). Neither one of us was a very good speller. While principals get by using a dictionary, second graders have spelling tests. My second grader was making himself sick worrying about his practice test.

As I walked down the hall to meet with my seven-year-old son, I pondered my words very carefully. While I was his elementary school principal I was, more importantly, his dad. We needed to have a dad talk.

As we spoke, I addressed the issue of spelling very quickly. I told him I thought that he was feeling bad because of the test, and I believed that he would feel better after the test was over. He agreed to stay in school, take the test, and see how things went. I agreed to pick him up after school to drive him home so we could have some alone time for a few minutes. David and Elizabeth would take the bus.

I thought about him and our predicament all afternoon. Spelling wasn't making him sick. His father, the principal, was. At the end of the day, after he had taken any test, I would ask "How many did you get wrong?" I focused on the negative. This day would be different.

When he got into the car that afternoon, I asked how he was feeling. "Fine," was his reply.

And then the moment of truth. "How many words did you get right on the spelling test?"

"16."

"16 out of 20. That's great. You only have four to work on. I'm sure that you'll do well."

That was it. Our big talk was over. We spent the remainder of the drive just talking about being a kid and things that were going on in his kid life.

That evening we had an open house in the middle school. It was the first big parent night of the school year. It was time for me to welcome everyone and tell them what a great year we planned for their kids. Most of "their kids" had been "my kids" in elementary school.

I arrived early so that I could make my "dot picture." It took me longer to put it in a frame than it did to make the picture.

I began my "speech" by sharing the picture and I placed it on the stage. I told them they could look at the picture if they got tired of listening to me. At the end of the presentation, I picked up my new picture and told them of my experience with Michael over the past three Wednesdays. I asked everyone to look at the picture and think for a moment, privately, about what they saw. I went on to say that the black dot on the picture represented the four words that Michael misspelled on his test. The white portion of the page represented the sixteen words that he spelled correctly and all the other positive things that had occurred for him in school that day.

While negative things are a part of life, I believe the good things outweigh the bad. I vowed to the parents that when I worked with their children, I would look at the positive first. I asked them to do the same. We have to examine the negative, but we don't need to dwell on it.

"Our children do so much more correctly than they do incorrectly. We need to celebrate the good things in life."

I made a promise to those in attendance that I would do my best to operate that way. More importantly, I promised myself that I would take my experience with Michael and his "spellitis disease" to heart. To see the glass as half-full rather than half-empty. I don't expect that any of the 200 teachers and parents remember my talk, the picture, or my promise. But I do.

I placed my "Michael picture" in my office and looked at it every day for the remainder of my years in Addison. I looked at it each day during my sixteen years in Britton-Macon, and I look at it each day as a part of my new life. I try to live by looking at the positive. I'm not always successful, but I always try. The things the black dot represents still appear in my life from time to time, but I choose to look forward and celebrate the good things.

I owe my outlook on life to my seven-year-old son. If not for his difficulty with spelling, I wouldn't have lived the life I have.

As for spelling, it's still a challenge for both of us. When it comes to life, he's become a wonderful man.

## Chapter 6

## The Marriage Rules

All three of our kids have always been social beings. David and Michael had girlfriends and Elizabeth had boyfriends. I was comfortable with that arrangement but knew that alternative choices were possible. I liked all the girls the boys dated. Elizabeth's choices were scrutinized more closely. I knew that when they were all out of the house, off to college, and on their own, the next guy or gal could be "the one." Since I was a boy at one time, I understood the intentions of boys. I wasn't comfortable with boys having intentions regarding my daughter.

The first Christmas break after all three kids were in college, David and Michael each brought a girl to the house. I liked them. I had known David's friend for some time; however, this was my first meeting with Michael's new girl. Both girls had "the look." I had seen "the look" in my youth. While I recognized "the look" on these two young ladies, I feared that both of my sons were oblivious to what was happening. After all they were still just boys at heart. I was more seasoned. It appeared to me that each of the girls might be focused on marriage and these two boys could be sitting ducks.

I sprang into action with an attempt to slow things down. I started by talking about how proud I was of all my kids. I never had to bail anyone out of jail, as far as I knew none of them were parents, and I believed that everyone was drug-free. And then I asked if I had ever told them *"the marriage rules."* I knew the answer before I asked the question. They couldn't have known the rules as I was making them up on the spot to slow the girls down and discourage thoughts of immediate nuptials.

Before you marry, you must follow these rules.

One – You must complete your degree.

My rationale for this was simple. Earning a degree before you get married is a lot easier. They had started on a path, and I wanted them to complete the journey. You shouldn't have to worry about providing for a wife, and perhaps children, while you are engaged in your studies. Ruth and I were paying most of their college expenses, but if you're on your own with a wife, you are going to be on your own with your college education. Complete independence comes with additional responsibilities.

Two – You must be twenty-four years old.

I chose the number 24 for a couple of reasons. I knew that if they completed their educations as planned, the age requirement would provide them with some additional alone (prior to marriage) time. Secondly, Ruth and I were 24 when we married so I wasn't making a rule that I hadn't followed.

Three – You must work in your
chosen profession for fifteen months.

Getting started on a career path is difficult. While you may have the greatest intentions, sometimes things don't work out. Fifteen months should be ample time to 1) determine if you've made a good choice and 2) start off on another path if things don't work out. You don't want to have a family without having a source of income.

Four – Your spouse must be employable.

It's not important that your spouse has a degree, but if the two of you decide that each of you is going to work, you each need a set of skills that will allow that to happen. If your spouse does earn a degree, she should consider following rule number three as well.

Five – You must be nice to each other.

Being in love and being nice can be two different things. You can love someone, but sometimes put your needs and desires above the one that you love, so it's important to avoid that pitfall by being nice to each other.

The marriage rules were developed in one, quick, spur of the moment conversation. They were created as food for thought. I knew that whether they were actually followed, or not, was to be determined. Life happens. That night I was just having fun thinking about what might be a good idea. I also knew that Ruth and I had followed rules 1-4 without a hitch. Rule five, perhaps the most important rule, has had its ups and downs but many more ups than downs.

In the end, all three children followed the rules. I believe rule following was more accidental than intentional. Rule #5 will always be a work in progress for everyone. David and Michael didn't marry either of the girls with "the look," but they did marry, and they chose wisely.

Of the two boys, David took the rules to heart. Ruth and I saw his college friends on a regular basis. Every once in a while, he would ask me to recite the rules for one of his friends. I'm not sure if he was asking me to provide a bit of entertainment for the guys, or if he recognized "the look" on one of this friend's girlfriend's face and was helping a buddy out.

# Chapter 7

# Three Toasts

I've had the opportunity to offer up several "toasts" at a dinner. My first took place when I was eighteen. I was the best man at my cousin Gene's wedding. Another followed when I was about to turn twenty-two and served as best man for my friend, Mitch. I was in my late forties when I last served that role. I've hosted dozens of social gatherings, offering welcomes and words of wisdom, but the three toughest were at the rehearsal dinners for each of my children.

David and Lindsay got married in Lindsay's parents' yard. It was a beautiful August day in 2004. The reception was held at Jackson Community College. About a hundred of their closest friends and family attended the wedding, and more than three hundred attended the reception. It was a big bash.

The rehearsal dinner was held the night before at Clark Lake's Beach Bar. The event was very informal. When I started to speak, I said, "I have the reputation of being something of a hard ass. The truth is, I'm more like an M-&-M candy on a hot July day. Thin, hard, outer shell and mush on the inside."

I cried before I started speaking and did so throughout my

entire toast. I did my best to control my emotions, but my oldest child, my first-born son, was getting married, and I just lost it. I had warned Ruth ahead of time too, "Just let me go on my own. I know I'm going to cry, but I want to get through this without your support." She had, and still has, a habit of trying to draw attention to herself by offering up some funny quip which allows me time to gather myself. I wanted to fly solo even if that meant sobbing while I did it.

As our kids were growing up, Ruth often spoke to them about the choices we make in life, and how each of them impacts us. Some are good and some are bad. I went on to speak about the choices that we all face. I explained that my most important choice was marrying Ruth because that choice led to the birth of our three children. I spoke of how proud I was of each of them, and the unique paths that each of them had chosen. My final remarks focused on the about-to-be married Lindsay and David.

We raised our glasses to the couple, and they have been living a full life ever since. They are a great duo, raising two wonderful children, and making it through both good and challenging times as one.

Mike and Kate had a destination wedding on the big island of Hawaii. They were married on the beach on the afternoon of October 2, 2009. Kate scheduled the time of the ceremony so that wedding pictures would coincide with the setting sun. It was beautiful.

It was terribly windy that day. Folding chairs were thrown about, ladies held down their dresses, and everyone marveled at how constant the strength of the wind remained. The minister offered up an explanation of the wind when she said, "The wind is the souls of those who have passed before us. They are arriving at the wedding." If that is indeed the case, we had hundreds of uninvited, but welcome, guests.

The prior evening, the wedding party and our extended family members gathered at our condo. We cooked food on the patio, played games in the house, and shared a grand time. When it came time to offer up a toast, I spoke once again, and cried through most of it.

I spoke of the relationship between Ruth and our grandson, Brady, who was five at the time. Ruth, Brady, and his sister, Eva had gone on several ice cream taste tests throughout the prior summer. Ruth often commented that she thought, "The best bite of an ice cream cone is the last one." One day, as the summer was drawing to a close, Brady handed Ruth the last bite of his cone.

When she asked, "Why are you giving this to me?"his reply was simple, but heartfelt. "Because I love you, Nana."

I concluded my toast with "True love is sharing everything, even the things that you'd like to save for yourself."

Six months later we gathered again for the wedding of my only daughter, Elizabeth. She and her husband, Sutton, celebrated their tenth anniversary a couple of days ago on April 3rd.

They were married in San Diego overlooking the Pacific Ocean. Although they lived there, this was another destination wedding for most of the attendees.

Like the prior two weddings, the rehearsal dinner was held the night before. We gathered at a house that Sutton's dad had rented for the weekend. It sat directly across the street from the wedding site. It featured the final of the three toasts that I offered up for my children. Lindsay and Kate placed bets on how long it would be before I started to cry. The over/under was five seconds. If you took the under, you won.

The more I spoke, the more I was able to compose myself. I started off by saying something like, "I've never liked any of the guys that Elizabeth dated. I saw them all as needy. She majored in psychology and has the skillset to help fix people, but I didn't want her to choose a mate that needed help. Each of the guys I met had a flaw that needed to be fixed."

About that time Sutton's grandmother spoke up and said, "Sutton doesn't need to be fixed."

I replied as quickly as she spoke, "But that's not the point. The point is, ***she*** doesn't think he needs to be fixed. ***She*** loves ***him*** just the way he is and that's good enough for me."

So here we are, fifteen plus years since the first of the three toasts. Our family of five has grown to ten. My greatest joy is that everyone likes everyone. It's one thing to love someone, but an entirely different thing to like them. I like and love them all.

## Chapter 8

# Nana and TGO

Ruth and I love being grandparents to our two grandchildren, Brady and Eva. While we love them and enjoy being with them, becoming grandparents was a challenge for both of us. We really weren't ready to become grandparents.

The issue was not associated with life's role of being grandparents, but rather with the thought that we both looked upon our own grandparents as being OLD. We weren't ready to be there. We didn't view ourselves as being OLD, but the thought of being grandparents brought OLD age into our lives and we weren't ready for its arrival.

Don't get me wrong. We loved our grandparents. I was lucky enough to have mine in my life for several years; but in my mind, they were always OLD. I wasn't prepared to get there yet.

Ruth and I discussed this on several occasions and decided if we weren't called Grandma and Grandpa that might help with the transition. Ruth explored a number of names. They were all very clever and interesting. None of them made her sound OLD. Most of our "name discussions" were lengthy and took place while driving in the car. She settled on Nana and that has worked well for her. Our two grandchildren refer to her as Nanee upon occasion, but that's just a nickname.

My choice was more difficult to determine. There just weren't a lot of options to explore. Brady and Eva's maternal grandfather, Larry, was going to be called Papa so that eliminated that option right from the start. I couldn't see confusing the kids with two Papas. My own grandfather was called Poppy, but he smoked a pipe, and I surmised the name came from his pipe smoking days. Being a non-smoker, Poppy was not an option.

One day I jokingly suggested I be known as The Great One. Ruth picked up on that and suggested the name TGO. That was the birth of my new name. I decided I would tell my grandchildren that TGO was my Indian name and that TGO was short for – The Great One. I, too, have been nicknamed by the grandkids, and I'm happy being referred to as TeGee when they're feeling frisky.

Nana and TGO love being grandparents. We hope all people, as they transition through life's journey, are as blessed as we are by having Brady and Eva in our lives. We are *very* happy we are able to be *active* grandparents. While we may be getting older, we don't feel OLD.

## Chapter 9

## Brady and B

I received a teddy bear from my dad on my first Christmas. He's not a handsome bear, but he's mine. We're celebrating our 71st Christmas this year. While he remains in Michigan, I am writing about him in Florida. Distance doesn't change anything.

I expect that I played with him when we were very young. The only verification that we spent time together in our youth is a photo. I believe we were about the same age. He's aged better than me and doesn't look much different today. He has the same pug-nosed face. His arms, legs, and neck can spin completely around. He's maintained his youthful flexibility but doesn't get out much anymore. He may have shrunk a bit and I don't believe that he ever bathed.

I bathe every day. Perhaps that's why I have wrinkled skin and he doesn't.

When each of my children was born, I bought a teddy bear for their first Christmas. David's has a look similar to mine, Elizabeth received a blonde bear with a bit of a shaggy look, and Michael's resembled the movie star, Winnie the Pooh. David's bear moved north with him to his family cottage at Twin Lake. I believe that

Elizabeth's and Michael's bears may be runaways as I haven't seen them in many years.

I didn't name my bear and I don't believe that David, Elizabeth, or Michael named theirs either.

When I was the elementary school principal in Addison, I was invited into a third-grade classroom to read a story. "Ira Sleeps Over" instantly became my favorite children's book. I read it to hundreds of students over the years. Each time I read it, I brought my bear to school and shared it with the students. I told them that my dad had given it to me on my first Christmas. I also shared that I had purchased a bear for my own three children for each of their first Christmases.

My grandson, Brady, celebrated his first Christmas thirteen years ago. I bought him a bear and he named it B. When Eva was born, I bought her a bear as well. B became an integral part of Brady's life. After a while, Eva's bear went off to live with Elizabeth's and Michael's.

B is from Las Vegas. I'm not sure if he was born there, but that's where Ruth found him. He's a polar bear and the first polar bear that we welcomed to our family. The only one for that matter. It was love at first sight.

Over the years, Brady has grown taller and more handsome. B is another story. He's lived a tough life. He's been slept on, puked on, peed on, and maybe pooped on. He's been through the wash several times and has had to be sewn back together on more than one occasion. He's traveled in backpacks and suitcases, been slung over shoulders, drug from room to room, ridden in cars, traveled on airplanes, and all in all lived a great, but exhausting, life.

Brady and B were constant companions. You never saw one without the other. Brady took B everywhere. They went from room to room together, visited friends and family in tandem, and spent the night together at grandparents.

One time Brady made a last-minute trip to spend the night with Ruth and me. As it became time for bed, Brady realized that B had been left behind. He panicked. He wasn't concerned for himself, but he worried about B. We decided we would call his dad. Dad promised that he would look after B, make sure that he had plenty to eat, and put him to bed on time. That's one of the few times during Brady's first several years that he didn't sleep with B.

I wanted Brady to like his bear and value it as much as I value mine. He exceeded my expectations. B took on a persona supplied by Brady. He turned out to be a loyal companion for a very special baby boy who has grown to become a wonderful young man. My hope is, should there be a son or daughter in Brady's future, that he purchases a bear for his child's first Christmas as I purchased one for him. I believe that it's a tradition worth sharing.

## Chapter 10

## Eva

When your children are born, your first concern is for their health. Do they have all their fingers and toes? If the answer is yes, the celebration begins. As your grandchildren are born, you take the same inventory.

Eva is my *grand*daughter with the emphasis on *grand*. She reminded me early on of my daughter, her Aunt Elizabeth. I thought they looked alike. While her looks have changed, her demeanor has followed the independent path of her aunt. She marches to her own drummer, and sometimes she's the whole band.

In her earliest years, Eva was into princesses. She loved them all and took on their persona from time to time. When she became one of the princesses, her dad, brother, or I became the male counterpart. We danced often and she preferred a dance that included a "dip." We twirled, she smiled, and my heart melted.

Early on in her make-believe world, she took on the role of Batman. When I corrected her and said she should be Batgirl, she became upset and insisted she be Batman. That's just how it was. I became Robyn. I had two capes made for her third birthday – one for Batman and one for Robyn. We often spoke to each other as our caped counterparts would speak to one another. It was great fun and full of love.

We have a large deck near the water on the lake where we live. The deck has served as a castle, a pirate ship, a dungeon, a magnificent house, and a simple cottage. Each location included a grand story that was developed on the spot and in the moment. All it took was our imaginations and a willingness to share our time with each other.

A few years ago, I took a "magic" class. Eva has joined me in the pursuit of magic. One of our card tricks involves the telling of a story while manipulating the cards. My story is always the same. It involves cowboys, Indians, and mountain lions. When Eva does the very same trick, her story is never the same. One time, it's lions, tigers, and bears. Another it's cows, sheep, and barns. While the characters differ from telling to telling, the outcome is always the same and the magic even more special.

Eva's interests are varied. She plays basketball, softball, sings, is an artist, a short order cook, a gymnast, a baker, and an equestrian, to name just a few. She's ambidextrous. (Or perhaps still a work in progress.) I've seen her write with her right hand and then switch to her left. While playing softball, she'll bat left-handed and switch to the right side for her next trip to the plate. Amazing.

Most of all, Eva is Eva. A few years ago, Ruth and I started taking our grandchildren on trips for their birthdays. We decided we would focus on experiences with Brady and Eva rather than things. Brady's trips are easy to plan. He wants to see all the baseball parks in the country, so we started down that path with him. Eva's varied interests make her a bit of a challenge.

Two birthdays ago, our daughter Elizabeth and her husband Sutton had recently moved to Flagstaff, Arizona. We decided to take both kids on the same trip to visit their aunt and uncle, take in the view from the top of Mount Humphrey, and enjoy a Diamondbacks game. I was talking to Eva a couple of weeks before the trip and I asked her if she was getting excited about her birthday trip. She told me it wasn't her birthday trip; it was Brady's. I reminded her that although it was early for her birthday (she's October and Brady's is June), August is right in the middle. "We're going to celebrate both birthdays at the same time, on the same trip." Her retort was priceless, "I'm not countin' it."

My reply was simple and to the point. "I'm payin, so I'm countin it." The trip was fantastic, and everyone had a great time.

I look forward to these trips for as long as she wants to travel with us. My guess is she'll "count it" if she has more of a say in where we go. That's how she rolls.

## Chapter 11

## Jackson James

When Ruth and I decided on names for our three kids, we wanted strong names we'd like both as their formal name and potential abbreviated version. David might become Dave, Elizabeth—Liz—and Michael–Mike. We both defer to the more formal David, Elizabeth, and Michael. That's how I plan to roll with young Jackson James. He's going to be Jackson for me.

Jackson was a name Kate favored right from the beginning. She and Michael considered Jack rather than Jackson. That's what Kate calls him. The scales tipped in favor of Jackson once his middle name was chosen. Jack James wouldn't cut it, so they opted for the longer version, Jackson James. James is in honor of my friend, James A. Marvin, who passed way too soon.

Jim Marvin followed the paths of my three children and loved them all. He grew closer to David and Michael, and we often discussed the career path of the boys as they grew into men with families of their own. There was a time when he and I discussed buying a golf course near Battle Creek. The complex featured an eighteen-hole course, a full-blown pro shop, banquet facilities that could accommodate up to three hundred guests, and a track of land set aside for condo development. Jim had a dentist friend looking for an investment opportunity, and the concept included Jim and I becoming partners. Michael had recently graduated from Michigan State's hospitality program. We envisioned him being the general manager of the place. In the end, we passed on the opportunity.

Jim's interest in Michael was centered upon the fact he deemed him to be a "solid investment." He often said, "If Michael starts his own business, I want in. I'd invest in him." They discussed the future and mutually admired their paths.

Jim was a good man who thought of others before himself. He willingly shared his time, advice, and wealth. He gave the gift of himself and was a friend to anyone who needed one. He made a difference. Most importantly, he did it without thought of personal gain or accolades.

I suspect Kate and Michael discussed all those things before taking the step to name their son after James A. If young Jackson James grows up to be anything like my friend Jim, the world will be a better place.

## Chapter 12

## Dear Kate

Young Jackson James is only forty-two days old, but he's already made quite an impact. If his arrival was anything like David's, Elizabeth's, and Michael's, you understand the meaning of love at first sight like no other time in your life. He wasn't here a moment ago, and now he is. Your life has changed forever.

I read online that the American version of Mother's Day was created by Anna Jarvis in 1908, and it became an official U.S. holiday in 1914. Her mother frequently expressed a desire for the establishment of such a holiday, and after her mother's death, she led the movement for the commemoration. Jarvis later denounced the holiday's commercialization and spent the latter part of her life trying to remove it from the calendar. She obviously failed.

Kate, you've learned that Jackson can literally pee on you, and you still love him. A parent's love is unconditional.

I'll avoid the common platitudes about mothers. You'll probably receive a card or two today. They'll address those attributes. But here's a few expectations that may come as a surprise.

When Jack is four or five, he'll gather a bouquet of dandelions or

Queen Anne's Lace. He may even pick a stray tulip or daffodil. Whatever he chooses for this first presentation will be the most thoughtful bouquet you'll ever receive. He'll present it because he loves you, and the first time you receive a bouquet may be a "just because" gift.

On May 12, 2030, nine-year-old Jackson will walk into your bedroom with a breakfast tray to surprise you. There'll be a homemade card on the tray and a stack of pancakes he made himself. They'll be doused in orange juice, because the glass tipped a bit during transport, but you'll love them just the same. He may add sprinkles to help celebrate the day. He'll be sure to include half of a banana, because he knows that's part of your daily routine. The kitchen will be a mess, but you won't care.

On your fifteenth Mother's Day, you'll receive a card signed by Jack but purchased by Michael. He'll be too cool to remember your day. That attitude will only last a year or two.

When he's twenty, Jack will be away at school somewhere. You'll look forward to his call, especially the part when he tells you he loves you. You both know it's true, but sometimes it's easier to say over the phone.

In between these milestones, you'll receive a mountain of cards, both homemade and store bought. You'll save them and put them in a folder along with poems and short stories he writes for school or the new love of his life. You may receive a set of handprints set in plaster of Paris and drawings of your family. Please note the three of you holding hands with Jack featured in the middle. You'll keep the special books he buys "just for you" and read his signature and personal dedication more often than the book.

For years I've thought Hallmark developed Mother's and Father's Day to sell greeting cards. And while it's true companies like this paid for Anna Jarvis's funeral, the true importance of today is we take time to reflect. We consider the journey and rejoice in those who help us make the trip.

Happy Mother's Day!

## Chapter 13

## March 30th

March 30, 1975, changed my life forever. Our first child, David, was born. Back in the seventies when a baby was born, it was potluck. There were no procedures for determining if your child was a boy or a girl or if they would have all their parts. You got what you got.

I was an advocate for Anthony and Elizabeth or Jennifer. If we chose to shorten Anthony, we could call him Tony. I envisioned him looking like the Oscar Meyer Wiener boy with dark curly hair. Tony would have suited such a face very well, but as Ruth pointed out there was no guarantee our son would have dark curly hair. Our child, no matter the gender, would be fifty-percent Dutch. There were not a lot of dark, curly haired Dutchmen roaming the streets of Kalamazoo.

We wanted a middle name too, so we discussed initials as well as names. Mine are R.A.T. and, although no one made fun of them, we knew name calling could always rear its ugly head. We reviewed each option, including possible nicknames, potential initial acronyms, and decided strong, traditional names would suit our family best.

Ruth liked Michael for a boy, but I vetoed it. Michael was the name of her last boyfriend, so I just said, "No." We both liked David, so we agreed that would be his name should our baby be a boy. We decided Elizabeth would work best if we had a daughter. Two years after David was born, we did indeed have our Elizabeth. Sixteen months after she was born, I had matured, and our Michael was born.

The decision to name our eldest David was a good one. We added the middle name of Anthony to honor my dad. Ruth's dad's name was Roelof, so there was no expectation that he'd be honored in our lineage. David Roelof doesn't roll off one's tongue, so we never really considered it.

Choosing names is a big deal. I was just hours short of being named Danny Lee. I'm grateful my parents had a last-minute change of heart and went with Robert Allen.

I believe David is happy with his name. The name has biblical roots and means "beloved." Although Ruth and I didn't discuss the origin or its meaning prior to his birth, it suits him well. After forty-seven years, we're happy with the name we chose, and the man he's become.

## Chapter 14

## The Hippies Are Gone

The hippies pulled out of town yesterday morning at 11:08. It's hard to believe that they were only here sixteen weeks. If you use a day planner, that's 112 days. All of you math geniuses out there know that converts to three months, two weeks, six days, fourteen hours, nineteen minutes and fifty-nine seconds. If your name is Jonesy, you've aged 2.35 years.

Time flies.

The hazmat team arrives at 8:00 a.m. on Monday morning. Ruth plans to clean up a bit before they arrive. I suggested just sealing off the area, but she wants to make sure the team is clear to enter safely.

Rather than bill them our standard $100-a-night "friends and family" fee, we've waived the entire $11,200. By the time we calculated the state and federal taxes, resort fee, cleaning fee, and booking fee, the entire bill would have exceeded $16,000. They're living on a budget, so we thought it best just to let it go.

I know what you're thinking. We could have paid off the house. But we're family and who knows when we might need to live with them for three months, two weeks, six days, fourteen hours, nineteen minutes, and fifty-nine seconds. (Ruth says, "When hell freezes over.")

Elizabeth, Sutton, and Jonesy came to Michigan last summer, arriving on June 30th. They bunked with us off and on for a couple of months before heading back west. They came to Florida last winter and lived near us for four months. They headed back to Jerome in early April and have been living with us ever since (three months, two weeks, six days, fourteen hours, nineteen minutes and fifty-nine seconds).

They've lived their lives in three-to-four-month chunks since April of 2018. They've outlined another chunk that will take them through October. They left yesterday for a couple of weeks in northern Michigan. The first will be in the Lower Peninsula, and then they'll be in the U.P. for a week. Ruth and I will join up with them a couple of times to make sure that they're still heading north. Mike and Kate are coming in from California to join us in Munising and Marquette. David and his crew are joining us there too. It will be a grand adventure.

After singing their way through the Upper Peninsula, they are heading west through Canada, down the west coast, and across to Arizona before spending the first two weeks of October in Mexico. They'll run around the southwestern United States through the end of October before landing in San Diego. They have job offers there, and I expect that they'll stay for a while.

I've confirmed some beliefs and learned a few new things while the three hippies have been hanging with us.

Sutton is a good man. He's solid. He lives a lifestyle that I could never follow, but it works for him, and more importantly, my daughter. He loves his music, is creative, knows how to cook, and eats more than any human I have ever met without gaining an ounce. It's a gift. He has a presence that makes others feel at ease.

He has taught me a few things on the computer, shared stories about growing up in California, and let me continue to beat him in golf. (He hits the ball a long way but never is really sure where it's headed.) I've taught him how to use power tools and to wear shoes, not sandals, when you climb a ladder to clean the gutters on a house.

Elizabeth is very much the same woman that left for California in the fall of 2001. I just know her better now. She has a strong set of beliefs, compassion for others, and is still trying to figure out what's next. Her last couple of years of high school, and then college, we saw each other but seldom spoke about the important stuff in life. She was always on her way to or from something like most people her age. (And exactly like me during my high school and college years.) She never really landed long enough for a truly meaningful conversation.

We've had more time to connect over the past year, and most of the time, we agree. We're also smart enough to avoid the topics that we know will bring about conflict. She is who she is, and I am who I am. We have common goals but have taken different paths to get where we're going.

Jonesy is another story. He's the same hair shedding, tail wagging, food snatching dog that he's always been. Spoiler alert. Ruth plans to make Jonesy a throw pillow from the dog hair that she's gathered in both Florida and Michigan. He's getting it for Christmas.

We've left him alone more in Michigan so more food has gone missing. He's gobbled a couple of loaves of bread, a half dozen donuts, and several cookies. He was bold enough to wolf down a couple of chicken legs while we still sat at the dining room table. He stealthily pawed them off the table as we sat and talked.

He whined a bit more whenever the kids left the house. I think that's in large part because he wanted to go fishing. Last summer he wanted to chase ducks and squirrels. This summer he learned to fish. He fished for hours and had a "catch-and-eat" mentality. The boy loves his sushi.

Friday evening, Sutton asked what my plans for Saturday were after they pulled out of town. I replied, "You mean after the dance?"

He looked at me quizzically. "Is Brady going to another dance?"

"No, I'm having a celebration dance."

"What are you celebrating?"

"Your departure."

The truth is, we'll miss them. All three. Ruth and I have lived differently with them around. We've traveled to more bars and honky-tonks than I can shake a stick at. We've memorized a couple dozen songs, drank more than our fair share of craft beer, and enjoyed living vicariously through, and with, the three hippies.

## Chapter 15

## A Father's Perspective

I'm going to a celebration next Saturday in California. Our daughter, Elizabeth, has published a book and it's making its public debut that day. *The Elephant on Aaron's Chest* is thirty-six pages long, contains 289 words, and took fifteen years to write. You can't rush perfection.

Elizabeth is a licensed clinical social worker in San Diego. She graduated from Addison Community Schools, earned her bachelor's degree at Western Michigan University, and her master's from the University of Michigan. What I know about the book, and her experience writing it, is "a father's perspective."

She talked about becoming a writer when she was in high school. I've saved several of her and her brother's compositions. They give me a look at who they were during their high school years. Some were given to me; some were just left behind when they headed off to college. I take a look back from time to time.

In her late twenties, as she was establishing her career as a social worker, she began talking about children's book ideas she developed. Some were serious, while others were a comical look at life through what she envisioned a child might see. They may have been glimpses of her own childhood. Only she knows for sure.

If you speak with Elizabeth about her book, she'll tell you she was inspired by her friend, Shayne. He was a childhood friend who grew up in our neighborhood. He played on a baseball team with her brother, David. I coached the boys. Shayne's father helped remodel our house at Lake LeAnn when we added our master suite. It still sports the windows, siding, and screened porch that he and his crew installed. His grandmother, Dee, once asked me for advice about publishing a children's book she had written. I worked with her for a brief time with no success.

Elizabeth had a crush on Shayne, and after they both graduated from high school, they dated for a time. They remained good friends even after they married others and Shayne had a son, Jaiden.

When she was getting serious about her writing, Shayne was in a dark place, and he told her he felt like there was an elephant on his chest. That became the focus of her book, and she asked Shayne, an artist, if he would illustrate it. He agreed and brought the two characters, Aaron and his elephant, to life with his drawings. During one of his darkest times, Shayne attempted suicide. He failed in his first attempt, sought help, started doing better, faltered, and succeeded in his second attempt. The book ground to a halt.

Her desire to publish gained momentum a few years ago. She sought advice from published authors, book publishing companies, joined writing groups, and honed each word, each page, until they were perfect. She needed an illustrator and reached out to a young man she had counseled who was also a talented artist. He agreed to do the work and spent more than a year in production. Arturo Lappara's drawings are spectacular.

*The Elephant on Aarons' Chest* is about a young boy who is struggling with his feelings which have taken on the form of an elephant. A friend recently asked the intended audience of the book. What age is it meant for? I didn't have a good answer for her as, although the book is about a young boy, I think it reaches across all ages.

When I was teaching, I used children's books and song lyrics with my students. I wanted them to see you could reach out to others and touch their souls with just a few well-chosen words.

I think each of us has an elephant traveling through life with us. Some settle in when life's pressures are too much. Children are sometimes challenged by making friends, attending new schools, overbearing bullies, learning a new skill, or the death of a loved one. Adults are confronted with financial challenges, marital strife, workplace turmoil, world headlines, and raising a family.

My elephant got heavy with the passing of my friend, Jim, and a few months later, my cousin Gene. While we may not rid ourselves of the negative feelings that seem to crush us, we can accept their presence, and learn to embrace them. Learning to understand ourselves, like Aaron, should be a goal for all of us.

I'm extremely proud of Elizabeth's accomplishment. I'm honored she chose her childhood name as her pen name. Even if this is the only book she ever writes, BZ Tebo will always be my favorite author.

## Chapter 16

## Courage

I received a book in March of 2005 from my daughter, Elizabeth. *Courage* was written by Bernard Waber. It's a picture book which explains there are all types of courage. She received a copy from the vice-president of the company she was working for at the time. During a presentation to his employees, he asked everyone to think of someone who had been a leader in their life. Elizabeth wrote a card for me to accompany the book. She explained she thought of me when offered the choice. I was flattered. It's one thing for your child to think this, but it's entirely different when they let you know. I'm fortunate my three have all expressed such a thought.

She also hoped I could find a creative way to use the book. When I retired in 2008, I bought a copy for each member of my staff. That was my creative usage. We read the book aloud with each member reading a new passage. I explained we were all going to need courage over the next several months. I was retiring, and they were getting a new leader. Both presented new challenges and would require courage.

Waber offers there are many types of courage. "There are

awesome kinds and everyday kinds. Courage is starting over. Being the first to make up after an argument. Sending a valentine to someone you secretly admire and signing your real name."

One of my third-grade teachers shared the book with her class and asked each to write an example of courage accompanied by a drawing. She assembled their work in a spiral-bound book and presented it to me. I ran across it while unpacking yesterday. The entries included these thoughts. *Giving instead of receiving. The first day of school. Not sneaking to look at your Christmas presents. Trying new things you were scared to do when you were a kid.* I think their observations were pretty insightful for a group of eight-year-olds.

The past fifteen months have tested everyone's courage. We've been asked to work together to fight an invisible enemy. The first several months offered the greatest challenges because it was so new. We were glued to our television sets and logged into social media to gain insight and direction. Each of us decided to follow the advice to mask up, socially distance, wash our hands frequently, and hunker down until we were told it was safe to move about. We didn't like it, but most of us followed the advice. We thought it best for the collective good.

Near the end of 2020, we heard the news of the successful development of a vaccine to ward off the virus. It was developed at "warp speed." Moving forward at such a pace required courage. Most were amazed that success came as fast as it did. Many are skeptical that it was developed too soon and are rightfully concerned about the potential for unknown consequences.

Ruth and I moved forward and received the vaccine based upon the recommendations we read and the urging of our elected leaders. We wanted to protect ourselves and be in a position to meet our grandson when he was born. We did our best to get near the front of the line. We understood there were some who had a negative reaction to the vaccine, but we mustered the courage to move forward just the same. After receiving it, our lives are a bit more normal. Ruth struggles with continuing to wear a mask, while I'm more accepting. We've done what we've done because we thought it best.

There's a new struggle with the virus that some will continue to debate for a long time. They don't trust the vaccine. They are concerned about the long-term effects and refuse to make the move. While I don't agree with that path, I respect their right to take it. I think an equally challenging struggle is the consequence of not receiving the vaccine. There may be reluctance by some to include the non-vaccinated in valued activities. Friends and family members with differing opinions could face the greatest challenge. That's the price they may pay for having the courage to follow their beliefs.

Elizabeth shared two examples of courage with me. They're written in the book she gave me. It's on display in my office, and I see it every day.

Courage is being a parent.

Courage is encouraging your family to follow their dreams, even when it takes them across the country.

I wouldn't want it any other way.

## Chapter 17

# A Priceless Gift

Last week, as we were preparing to head north for the summer, Ruth ran across an old Mother's Day gift from David. He gave it to her when he was in elementary school. It's a coupon book she's never used. She brought it north, hoping to redeem a coupon or two. They read as follows:

- Good for one free room cleaning (doesn't include the closet)
- Good for one free hug
- Good for one day of no arguments (He included his sister, BZ, and brother, Mike, in the coupon, making it a gift from all three.)
- Good for one free car wash
- Good for one free yell

The artwork is particularly endearing. It's taken from David's "stick figure period." I think all young people go through such a time. It's a tried-and-true way to express yourself in a medium that has universal appeal.

Most parents have received similar gifts from their children. They're the ones that mean the most. While the coupon book didn't require a large monetary investment, it did take some time to create. Each coupon expresses a gesture that David thought his mom would appreciate. And when it's all said and done, parents appreciate their children's time more than anything else. It's a priceless gift from the heart.

# Chapter 18

# Trust

We all know the "trust game." One guy stands erect, crosses his hands in front of his chest, falls back, and trusts that his friend will catch him as he falls. The test is "do you trust your friend" to catch you? Over the years I've been comfortable being the catcher, but I've never been the guy who "trusts the catcher." I know – it's a flaw.

We are asked to trust many people in our everyday lives – police, politicians, doctors, and repairmen for all kinds of products – cars, computers, appliances, and anything that has a switch or a gizmo. The list is endless.

The greatest example of trust that I am privy to involves my wife, Ruth, and one of her students. If this isn't the greatest example of trust that you've ever heard, I'll let you be my "trust fall catcher."

Ruth taught for the Adrian Public Schools for several years. They originally hired her to teach one hour a day. The second semester they increased her work load to a half day and the following year she was full-time. She built the program because she was good at what she did. Her original assignment was home economics. (That's long gone and a terrible decision) They added interior design, independent living, child development, and sex education.

Most classes were a semester long and the demand for her program grew. She went from one class to two full-time teachers within a period of three years. Phenomenal growth.

She planned many of her lessons at home and I expect that our three "students" have a number of stories in their memory banks about our dinner discussions. While I would ask "what if" questions i.e. "What would you do if someone offered you a ride at the bus stop?" Ruth had "show and tell." She spoke of STDs and had pictures with stories to back up her presentation. She was very specific in her use of language. Boys have a penis, not a pecker. Girls have a uterus and vagina, not a hoochee. Every discussion came with graphs and diagrams. That was our dinner table life.

One summer afternoon, while I was still the elementary principal in Addison, I answered our phone. A male voice asked if Mrs. Tebo was home. The voice sounded young and anxious. I told him "yes" and called Ruth to the phone. I stayed in the room and listened to Ruth's end of the conversation. As the telephone call developed, I could tell that the young man needed help and the person he chose to turn to for guidance was his teacher.

Ruth: "Hello?"

Anxious boy: …

Ruth: "Oh, hello, anxious boy, how are you? Are you having a good summer?"

Anxious boy: …

Ruth: "Yes, I remember our discussion of condoms."

Anxious boy: …

Ruth: "Yes, sometimes they break and if they do pregnancy is always a concern."

Anxious boy: …

Ruth: "Well, that doesn't necessarily mean that she's pregnant. But it is possible."

Anxious boy: …

Ruth: "If she is pregnant then I believe that it would be best if she told her parents. She may want you to help with that discussion. The two of you should talk about that and decide what the best approach would be."

Anxious boy: ...

Ruth: "I would wait until you know that she is pregnant. There's no reason to cause concern with her parents until you know that. If she's not sure then the best thing to do is to have her go to her family doctor to confirm the pregnancy. If she doesn't have a doctor, I can help you find one. How long has it been since her last period?"

Anxious boy: ...

Ruth: "How long has it been since you had sex?"

Anxious boy: ...

Ruth: "This happened thirty minutes ago? The condom broke thirty minutes ago?"

Anxious boy: ...

Ruth: "If this just happened, I don't think you need to do anything right now. You both need to relax. Chances are she's not pregnant and worrying about it could cause her to miss her period."

Anxious boy: ...

Ruth: "I'm glad you called. Just relax. Time will tell if you have anything to worry about. You can call me any time.

Anxious boy: ...

Ruth: "You're welcome. Good-bye."

As I listened to Ruth's words, a picture formed in my mind. I saw a naked, teenage boy sitting on the edge of a bed with a broken condom in one hand and a telephone in the other. I saw a young girl wrapped in a sheet in the fetal position, listening to her boyfriend seek advice from his teacher. The boy hung on every word that the teacher spoke. At the most vulnerable time in his life he needed help and the person that he trusted most was Mrs. Tebo.

If that's not the greatest example of trust you've ever heard, you can be my "trust fall catcher."

Oh, I almost forgot. She wasn't pregnant. The two married, but not each other. Every once in a while I read about the boy and the successful man he has become. I expect that he remembers that call and Mrs. Tebo. After over thirty years, I know I do.

## Chapter 19

# The Wesco Gas Station

The summer between my sophomore and junior year at Western, I bought a 1967 Mustang convertible. It was silver with a black top. If I was any cooler after that purchase, I would have been twins. My parents helped me look for the car, arrange for the loan, and added the Mustang to their car insurance. My car payments were $104.00 a month. I made them to my mom because she co-signed my loan at the bank.

A couple of months after school started back at Western, I got a call from my mother. My car insurance had been raised to $1,000 every six months. It seems that police officers had a sixth sense regarding silver Mustang convertibles with black tops, and they didn't care how cool the driver was. They stopped me on more than one occasion that summer, and the points added up. As far as the insurance company was concerned, I was a bad risk.

I couldn't afford the increased insurance rates, so my dad struck a deal with me. He'd drive the Mustang to work, and I could drive his 1963 Ford 500 Galaxie until my insurance rates dropped. We expected this would be six months to a year. I was stuck. If I wanted to drive a car, this was my best option. I drove the Galaxie back to Western after the Thanksgiving break. I continued to pay for the Mustang.

Later that winter, I drove the Galaxie to pick up the girl I was dating at the time. We had begun dating my senior year of high school and our courtship continued into my junior year of college. She was attending nursing school in Cadillac. She was going to go to a fraternity dance at Western with me.

The primary road between Cadillac and Kalamazoo is US 131. The Galaxie broke down south of Grand Rapids and north of Kalamazoo. I didn't know what was wrong, but I knew it was bad. I managed to pull the car off the road. It was early evening, dark, and cold. I got out and flagged a car down by standing in the middle of the highway. The guy was going to hit me or stop.

I explained my problem and asked for a ride to the next town. I had no idea where we were, but I knew that we needed help. He invited us in, and we trusted that he would drive us to safety.

There's a Wesco Gas station just east of 131 on M-89 in Plainwell, Michigan. 131 is the primary dividing line between the rival towns of Otsego and Plainwell. He dropped us off there and bid us farewell.

I didn't know anything about where I was. The station attendant explained that the only tow-truck in town belonged to a man at a repair shop that was closed for the evening and wouldn't open until the following morning. "Your car will have to sit for the night." And so, it did.

He let me use the phone to call my roommates. I didn't know if anyone was home, so all I could do was hope. I made the call and Jim answered. I told him my story and asked if he would pick us up. "Where are you?," he asked.

"Some podunk town north of Kalamazoo called Plainwell. It's right off 131."

Jim arrived about forty minutes later. I found out the next day that the rear axle on the Galaxie was broken and needed to be replaced. I called my dad, shared the news, and after several questions he ok'd the repair.

My girlfriend and I went forward with our plans for the weekend. She returned to Cadillac a couple of days later via a carpool. People on college campuses shared ride information on bulletin boards in the student union, and that's how she got home. That was early in the winter of 1968.

I was engaged to that girl just before or just after the car broke down. We were engaged for a few months before she moved to Grayling to complete her degree. Once she landed there she became interested in another guy and she dumped me. Life throws curveballs every once in a while. This was one of mine.

In August of 1969 I received a phone call from Mr. Floyd Hindbaugh. He wanted to know if I was available to interview for a teaching job. It was a couple of months after I had graduated with my teaching degree. I had applied for dozens of jobs all over the state. I was willing to go anywhere.

Mr. Hindbaugh identified himself as the principal of the Plainwell Junior High School. "We're located just off 131 north of Kalamazoo."

"Yes, I know. I stopped at the Wesco Gas Station several months ago."

"Great. Can you be here Tuesday evening about 7:00 p.m.?"

"Yes. I'll be there. Thanks for the call."

Small world.

I got the Mustang back several months before that August interview. It went well, and I was offered a job before I left that night. I would be teaching six sections of seventh grade English, or two sections of geography and four sections of English. Mr. Hindbaugh asked if I had a preference. "Yes, I'd prefer the geography and English assignment."

He told me that he had another teacher coming in later that

evening, and "If she's certified for geography, I'd like you to take the English assignment. We don't have any male English teachers."

She wasn't, so I got the split assignment.

I taught eight great years in Plainwell. I made a lot of new friends, a million memories, and met my wife.

I also met a man, R. Lou VanBruggen, who I found to be the most intimidating man I've ever met. He owned his own construction company, served on the local school board, was a church deacon, a good golfer, and took a no non-sense approach to life. He and his wife, Kate, owned property in the area. Lou developed some of it and held some as investments.

One of the parcels had a total of forty acres adjacent to US 131. When the State decided to expand that stretch of road, he sold them part of the land. When the utility company decided to extend the power lines along the highway, he sold them a right of way. Lou couldn't foresee those opportunities, but they came his way anyway.

A farmhouse that stood on the northeast corner of the acreage was the focal point of the property. Lou, Kate, and their three daughters moved into the house in 1955. There was a single bedroom downstairs and the three girls shared three bedrooms with a single heat source on the second level. The lone bathroom was on the first floor, so the girls thought long and hard before making a dash downstairs on cold winter nights.

In the early 60s, Lou sold the bulk of the property so that a new community hospital could be built. The site included a couple of doctors' offices and eventually housed a dentist's office too. The new Pipp Hospital has served Plainwell and the surrounding area since then.

In 1964, Lou moved the farmhouse three hundred and sixty yards south across a field, through the developing hospital site, to a street that he had laid out called Benhoy. Once the house was moved, he added a family room and a garage. He didn't bother to add another heat run to the second story. By now his oldest daughter,

Shirley, had married and the two youngest, Ruth and Kathy, were in high school. I expect that he figured that since the girls had survived the circumstances as long as they had, a couple of more years wouldn't hurt them.

He sold the plot of land where the farmhouse stood to a company out of Muskegon, Michigan. The company built a Wesco Gas Station on the site. About four years later my girlfriend and I found ourselves at that station after my dad's 1963 Ford Galaxie 500 broke its rear axle. At some point in the past fifty plus years, Wesco moved one block east, and an Admiral Gas Station now occupies the site.

Life is full of unexpected twists and turns. I was engaged twice in my life. My first lasted several months and the second several hours. My first fiancé and I landed at the Wesco Gas Station where the home of my second fiancé once stood. If the man who picked us up after the car broke down would have turned right at the exit to head west towards Otsego instead of left towards Plainwell, my life may have turned out differently.

I met Lou and Kate's second daughter, Ruth, at the Plainwell Junior High. The hometown girl was hired the same summer as me. We eloped in the fall of 1971 and were pronounced "man and wife" twenty-two hours after I asked her to marry me. I spent a lot of time in the farmhouse that was moved from the site that became the home of Plainwell's Wesco Gas Station.

Shortly after we were married, we spent three weeks during our first winter with Lou and Kate while we remodeled the lower flat of a house that I owned. The upstairs bedrooms still had a single heat run, so I thought long and hard before venturing down to use the single bathroom at night.

Living together provided me the opportunity to learn more about Lou. He loved his family above all else and wanted to ensure that anyone who ended up with one of his daughters was worthy of her. I passed the test.

Looking back, the odds of me stopping at a gas station with one fiancé and marrying a second from the exact same plot of land have to be astronomical, perhaps a gazillion to one. But then again – it's a small world.

# Chapter 20

# Tegestology

Ruth is a tegestologist. She hasn't always been one. Her compulsion began like most. She had one and then another. She could have walked away, but she chose not to. Addiction is difficult to handle on your own and there are no support groups for tegestologists.

She came down with the affliction twenty-five years ago after a night at THE BOB, AKA Big Old Building, in Grand Rapids. It was a new venue, and she was attracted to the name. We didn't know it, but by the time she walked out the door, she was hooked. Once she started, she didn't have the power to quit. One led to another, and when the kids became aware of her compulsion, they fed her more and more. Some of her friends contributed as well. If the server in a restaurant or bar doesn't supply her, she'll come right out and ask for one.

Some might call her something else, but that's the name you give to people who like to collect beer coasters. Tegestology is a term coined from the Latin word "teges." It refers to a mat and is defined as the practice of collecting coasters. You would actually be quite surprised to see how many tegestogists are out there. It's not the hardest thing to collect, as beer coasters are available in most bars and honkytonks.

She collected dozens when we attended our son-in-law's performances in California, Florida, and Michigan. She collected several more when we started following our daughter-in-law, Lindsay, AKA Rozlyn Heart, and her singing career. Ruth has written notes on some to commemorate their addition to her collection while others have just been tossed in the pile. We've got hundreds in each of our homes and there's no end in sight. I expect she'll add hundreds more.

Fortunately, she hasn't had to drink a beer for every coaster in her collection. She's president of the short-hitters club. She's a one and done kind of gal, so requiring her to drink a beer to receive a coaster would have placed a huge damper on the project. She's content to sip on a glass of water with a lemon.

I'm happy Ruth is a tegestogist. She could have been a labeorphilist, collector of beer bottles (too much space), or a sucrologist, collector of sugar packets (possible ant infestation). I had a fraternity brother, Mike, who collected beer cans. He built a wall of aluminum in one of our apartments that rivaled the Great Wall of China. I didn't know it at the time, but he was a breweriana. Heck, my mother was a deltiologist and she lived to be ninety-three.

Ironically, I posted this story six days prior to Ruth's accident.

## Chapter 21

# Time

Time is a funny thing. When we're young time passes very slowly. Our next birthday and Christmas seem like they'll never come. Summer vacations are about the only "time" of the year that time passes quickly.

I was going through some old school documents from my education career and ran across the following story. I don't know the author, but it wasn't me. I've never been this insightful.

---

### *What is a Grandmother?*

*A grandmother is a lady who has no children of her own. She likes other people's little boys and girls. A grandfather is a man grandmother. He goes for walks with the boys and they talk about fishing and tractors and stuff like that.*

*Grandmothers don't have to do anything but be there. They are old, so they shouldn't play hard or run. Instead they drive us to the market where the mechanical horse is and have lots of dimes ready. They never say "Hurry up."*

*Usually grandmothers are fat, but not too fat to tie your shoes. They wear glasses and funny underwear. They can take their teeth and gums off.*

*It is better if grandmothers don't typewrite or play cards, except with us. They don't have to be smart, only answer questions like, "Why do dogs chase cats?"*

*Grandmothers don't talk baby talk like strangers do because it's hard to understand. When they read to us they don't try to skip pages, and they don't mind if it's the same story over again.*

*Everybody should try to have a grandmother, especially if you don't have a TV, because they are the only grown-ups who have time.*

---

Time. Everybody has some, but we really don't know how much. Most of us want more than we have, and yet, we don't always use it wisely.

I've thought about time a lot for the past several days. I've decided that the most important thing about time, no matter how much you may have, is that you should share yours with people you love. Do things rather than buy things. Be positive even if positive is hard. And most of all, make a difference.

# Section Two

## Family and Friends

## Chapter 22

## 500 Chunks

This is my five-hundredth blog. When I began writing in November of 2017, I had one goal; share stories of my life so one day my grandchildren would have a better understanding of their extended family. It's morphed over the years into a collection of thoughts and observations.

I'd estimate I've written about 320,000 words, well short of *War and Peace's* 587,287 or *The Bible's* 783,137. If I continue at my current clip, I'll catch *War and Peace* when I'm seventy-nine and *The Bible* about four years later. My writing isn't about length but rather, longevity.

I do a lot of pondering while driving, and the other day, I decided most of us live our lives in chunks. Blocks of time spent with a common purpose. Some last years, some a few months, while others are made up of bits and pieces.

The first big chunk is childhood. You learn about sharing, taking turns, being cared for, and caring for others. During adolescence, we begin to develop our sexual self with a series of physical, psychological, and social transitions. And while many adolescents believe they know everything, they don't. When I exhibited such an attitude, my mom called it "getting too big for my britches."

Somewhere along the way we develop our independence. We make a series of decisions that will impact us forever. We decide if we're going to continue our formal education, join the military, enter the world of work, or continue to mooch off our parents. All such decisions require a plan of action. Luck may have some minimal effect, but things happen because of the choices we make.

When I was getting ready to retire, I wondered what I would do to fill my days. I had met a retiring teacher a couple of years prior, and when I asked what she planned to do for the next thirty years, she said "read." Although I didn't say it aloud, I thought reading as a single purpose might get boring after a while.

I was fortunate to land a consulting gig that took a large portion of my time and expertise for the first thirteen years of my retirement. I met new people, helped students explore career opportunities, and developed a network of business associates, but I knew it wouldn't last forever, so I started this blog. Writing keeps my brain moving. I'm constantly amazed by what I recall once I turn it on. It's a fun way to share my retirement years.

I'll continue to share chunks of my life as long as I think I have something worth sharing. I'll write about things that interest me and, hopefully, you. If you learn something new, or rekindle a lost memory of your own, I've done my job.

# Chapter 23

## It's Gonna Rain Again

Once, several years ago, during my elementary school principal days, I received a phone call from a friend and new school principal. He needed my advice. He was the K-12 principal in a small school district. Students were housed in two buildings.

On this particular day, it was raining. My friend, Dave, had two recess aides who supervised students during the elementary school's lunch and recess. When inclement weather forced students inside, their supervision was a greater challenge because students were confined to their rooms rather than having the opportunity to play outside. Both aides had called in "sick" and no substitutes were available. This meant that Dave would have to supervise students to ensure that his teachers were granted their contractual "duty-free lunch/recess."

Students in the secondary school building started lunch prior to the elementary school. Dave made it a practice to be in this building during the lunch hour. True to form, Dave was in the high school at the beginning of lunch. His plan to report to the elementary school in time for their lunch hour was interrupted when a food fight broke out in the high school. He quickly called his elementary school secretary, described his dilemma, and directed her to seek the elementary school teachers' help by having them supervise their own students during lunch and recess while he remained in the high school.

After dealing with the high school food fight, Dave went back to the elementary school and learned that the teachers had not done as he had hoped. Students went to lunch, supervised by the school secretary, and returned to class for an unsupervised indoor recess.

Dave was furious. He called an emergency staff meeting to begin immediately after school dismissed. He called me ten minutes before the meeting was to begin. Dave described his situation and sought my advice. He couldn't believe that this staff could be so unresponsive – so irresponsible. How could they place their personal needs, and contractual benefits, above the needs and safety of their students?

My advice was simple. I pointed out that he didn't truly have all the information that he needed to deal with the staff appropriately. He didn't know what the secretary had said to the teachers. Had she asked for their help on his behalf or simply told them that they must stay with their students? What words did she use and what was her tone? We explored a number of unanswered questions. One thing was clear. He was upset and he was going to let everyone know.

Before he hung up, I asked him to take a deep breath, think of the precedent that he was about to set and to remember....

No matter what you choose to say, or how you say it, *it's gonna rain again.*

My point? No matter what you do in life, what course of action you take, similar situations will arise, and you need to consider that fact. How you react to one situation will be scrutinized when the next one arises. In Dave's case, he will want his teachers to help him down the road. If he alienates people, they will be less likely to help him when the next problem arises. He can let them know that he is disappointed in their lack of help this time without degrading them. He shouldn't let his initial anger affect the course of action he takes. Like I said, *it's gonna rain again.*

## Chapter 24

## Ma and Pa Tebo

My dad referred to his parents as Ma and Pa. I knew them as Grandma and Grandpa Tebo. George Gabriel Tebo was born in 1875 and Mary Christine Ritter eleven years later.

They raised a family of six girls and one boy. The girls were Nettie, Katherine, Elizabeth (Dutch) Bernadette (Bern), Julia (Jewel) and Gertrude (Gert). The lone son, Tony, was born on October 17, 1919.

Grandma and Grandpa Tebo lived in Mt. Clemens on Barbara Street. Their house was a few hundred steps from Shadyside Park. Shadyside's south boundary was the Clinton River.

Grandpa Tebo was the supervisor of the forty-acre park. He also ran a sand scow in the river up to Lake St. Clair. The flat bottomed boat was used to dredge the river bottom for sand.

Dad worked with Grandpa on the sand scow. There was no payment for his service. He helped him just because he was his father. Sometimes Dad fished the river. Fishing amounted to tossing a stick of dynamite into the river and collecting the fish when they floated to the top.

I remember visiting the house on Barbara Street a few times. The backyard featured a set of wooden stairs leading up to the small back porch. There was a vegetable garden and a grape arbor. The tomatoes, beans, squash, peppers, radishes, potatoes, and carrots were harvested and eaten fresh or canned. The grapes were used to make jelly and juice. Grandpa tended the garden and Grandma did the canning.

Canned goods, and Grandpa's cash, were stored in their Michigan basement. Grandpa lost much of his money when the banks failed during the depression, so he never returned to the banks. He kept his money in jars, counted it regularly, and trusted no one.

They had a chicken coop near their garden. The chickens provided eggs and fresh meat. The lone rooster provided company for the chickens.

The back door led directly into the kitchen. The kitchen stove was huge. (And if my memory is correct, it was a wood burner.) Everything served in this home was made from "scratch." Grandma made noodles, baked her own bread, delicious cakes, and top of the line cinnamon buns. The kitchen table served as her pastry board. She sprinkled it with flour, rolled and cut her dough, and made delicious homemade magic.

The main room in the house featured a "davenport" and two rocking chairs. Each of the elders sat in one. Grandpa chewed tobacco and used an old tobacco can as a spittoon. Straight back chairs were moved from the kitchen table to provide extra seating when guests arrived. There was a large metal floor grate that helped provide air circulation for the coal fired furnace. The front of the house had a long enclosed porch. There was a daybed and dozens of family pictures displayed on side tables that lined three sides of the porch.

Most of my memories of visiting the house included only our family. I was eight and a half when Grandpa passed. My sister, Sharron, was three years younger, and Jackie was twenty months. Some of our family pictures of our visits feature my Aunt Gert's three daughters, Jean and the twins, Gail and Gwen, so I know that others joined us.

My dad told me that his older sister, Katherine, loved me like her own child. She was ill and lived her last few weeks with her mom and dad in the house on Barbara Street. She stayed in the daybed on the front porch. When we visited I hopped into bed with her and took a nap. I was three years old when she passed, and I have no memory of her other than those shared by my dad.

My Aunts Dutch, Bern, Jewel, and Gert were loud, gregarious women. They smothered me with kisses whenever I saw them. They loved their brother, and then in turn, his children. Their hugs were full blown circle the wagon embraces. Once they took hold, there was no release until they decided to let go. I tried to hide from them behind my mom in my youth but miss them all as an adult. It was a group of ladies that didn't hide their feelings. You always knew where they were and how they felt.

I know nothing of Nettie except for what I have been told. She was the oldest child and she died when my father was fourteen. She spent her last days in the daybed on the front porch as the next oldest sister, Katherine, would years later.

The day before she passed, Grandpa took my dad aside and told him to go into the next room to say good-bye to Nettie. Grandpa knew that his daughter would not live much longer. He also knew that Tony should know the truth about Nettie.

"Nettie is not your sister. She's your mother."

Biology was one of the areas of study during my junior high school science classes. One of our assignments was to select one of several topics supplied by the teacher and develop a comprehensive report based upon biology. I chose to study twins.

We had several sets of twins on both sides of our family. My mom had two uncles, Henry and Ephraim, who represented her side. My dad's side had several: Gail and Gwen, Lynn and Leslie, and a brother/sister pair whose names escape me. During my study I learned that there were two types of twins: identical and fraternal. Biology books will tell you the difference between the two.

*Identical twins are those who originate when only one sperm cell fertilizes one egg. This zygote (the egg along with the sperm cell) divides into two, forming two embryos with the same genetic material. This results in two identical siblings that are born at the same time.*

*Fraternal twins are those produced by the fertilization of two eggs by two sperm cells. The result is two siblings that may be similar, or very different, who are born at the same time.*

We have both types of twins in our extended family.

My study indicated that it was possible, but highly unlikely, that fraternal twins can be born at two different times.

I researched trends and birth order. When I learned that my dad was one month older than his sister, Gert, I asked my mom if Dad and Aunt Gert were fraternal twins. She said, "No."

That's the day that I learned about Tony Jerome.

Tony Jerome was a thirty-year old bachelor who lived in what would now be called a studio apartment above a movie theatre in Mt. Clemens. Sixteen year old Nettie sold movie tickets in the theater. That's how they met. I don't know how long they knew each other or how they explained Nettie's pregnancy to Grandpa Tebo. I've been told that Tony wanted to marry Nettie but Grandpa wouldn't allow the union.

Grandma Tebo was pregnant with her sixth child when this occurred. The two babies, Anthony and Gertrude, were born within a few weeks of each other in the fall of 1919 and raised as brother and sister.

That's the story that my mother told me when I asked if my dad and Aunt Gert were twins. I spoke with my dad about it after hearing from my mom. The only other detail he added was that Nettie died the day after he learned that she was his mother. "I helped Pa dig a grave for Nettie the day she died."

Nettie married another, closer to her age, a few years after my dad was born. His last name was Rondeau and I never met him. If there were daughters born to the couple, I don't remember them. Two sons were born. Frank and George were my dad's half-brothers. My sisters and I met these men, but no mention of the relationship was ever discussed. They were included at some, but not all, family gatherings. I knew them as friends of the family.

All of my aunts were no-nonsense women. They told it as they saw it. One Saturday morning when I was fifteen Dad drove me to Aunt Bern's house to "wash her kitchen walls." My Aunt Dutch had hired me to provide the service for Aunt Bern. My dad was just my chauffeur.

The gathering was large that morning. My Grandma Tebo was living with Aunt Bern and her husband, Uncle Gene. Both my Aunt Dutch and Aunt Gert were there. One of the Rondeau boys showed up with his wife. My Aunt Bern was baking cakes while I washed walls and the remaining members of the clan sat around the kitchen table and reminisced. I started my job by washing the ceiling and then moved from wall to wall. The table setters adjusted the seating as I moved around the room.

At one point in the conversation the Rondeau wife said something like, "Tony's not really your brother." to the gathering of girls. They turned on her and attacked full force. "He's our brother and will always be our brother!" The Rondeau wife protested, and my Aunt Bern went after her like a lioness about to finish off her prey. My Uncle Gene grabbed Bern and held her tightly. If he hadn't, I'm sure that Aunt Bern would have wiped the floor with her.

That's the only time I was present when my dad's family relationship was openly discussed. Tony was their brother. End of discussion.

Later in life I had the opportunity to "baby sit" my dad. That's what he called it. He could no longer drive his car and upon a few occasions I spent the weekend with him while my mom visited relatives out of state. We never stayed home during our time together. We played cards at the senior center, drove to Windsor to play blackjack in the casino, or drove to visit one of my two Uncle Harry's and their wives. (His sisters had all passed.)

Dad shared stories of his family during our rides in the car. He told me that Tony Jerome had a reputation of being mixed up with a rough crowd. He also said that he had heard that he had been "shot to death near the Detroit River during the 40s." That's it. That's all he shared.

During one of our rides he asked to go to the St. Peters Church Cemetery in Mt. Clemens. We only went once. We looked for, and located, the grave that he had helped dig for Nettie over sixty years prior. We also visited the graves of Ma and Pa Tebo. They are buried a couple of hundred yards from their oldest child.

On our ride home that afternoon we spoke briefly of Grandpa Tebo and his younger brother, Art. I grew up thinking that they were the only two siblings in the Tebo family. He spoke of George and Art's other brothers and sisters. When we got home, I asked that he write their names on a piece of paper for me. He did, and I still have the paper. But that's a story for another day.

## Chapter 25

# Margaret and Harrison

I always considered my mom's parents, Margaret and Harrison (AKA Poppy), to be my rich grandparents and my dad's my poor ones. I knew nothing of their income other than the fact that Grandpa Barner had his own business, and Grandma Barner wore red nail polish. She's the only woman who I knew that wore nail polish all of the time. She wore a mink stole in the winter and the mink still had its eyes and claws. Grandpa wore a suit to most gatherings and smoked a pipe with cherry blend tobacco. They were always well dressed. That all seemed rich to me.

While many of the women that I knew wore "house dresses," I never saw Grandma Barner in one. Instead, she had a "maid" that cleaned her house each Friday. I met two of them – Sadie and Lola. They were paid a wage, lunch, and bus fare. If we happened to be around for lunch, we ate in the dining room and Sadie or Lola ate in the kitchen. We ate the same food – just in different rooms. Before mom learned to drive, she took my sisters and me on the train from Royal Oak to Detroit and Grandma picked us up at the train station. We always made the trip on a Friday, and that's how I was introduced to Sadie and Lola. Grandma served fried fish and fried corn bread on those Friday dinners because Dad and Mom were raising us as Catholics. It's the only time that I've had corn bread prepared that way, and I loved it.

While many grandmothers baked cookies, ours painted in oils and embroidered elaborate works. She taught my cousins and me how to embroider as well. She began her painting with "painting by numbers" and then moved on to painting beautiful pieces of china. They are wonderful pieces of art that even an untrained eye like mine can appreciate.

They moved to another home in Detroit on Troester. Grandpa bought the house from a family friend. The house had a fire in the upper apartment and their friends lost their son and daughter-in-law because of smoke inhalation. The friends didn't want to live in the house any longer, so they sold it to Grandpa and Grandma and they had the home repaired. The house had two built-in safes. The largest one was located in a cupboard in the walk-in pantry and the second was in the living room behind a false piece of floor trim. I didn't know anyone with a safe, and they had two. This confirmed their wealth for me.

Not long after they moved from one house to the other, my mom received a phone call from Grandpa early one December morning. Grandpa awoke in the morning and Grandma had passed during the night. They determined that she died because of a heart attack.

One key memory that sticks with me was that Grandma was a fan of an afternoon game show whose name I can't recall. The show provided rewards to home contestants that had dollar bills whose serial numbers matched those shown on the show. While helping Grandpa reorganize the house, Mom found one hundred one-dollar bills in a drawer of an end table that set next the Grandma's favorite chair.

She was only fifty-nine when she died. I was eleven. Our family Christmas gathering in 1958 was a somber one. That first Christmas night was interrupted by a "no heat" call from one of Grandpa's customers. He wanted every family to enjoy Christmas night so we loaded up his truck, and my cousin, Gene, and I joined "Poppy" on his call.

Our 1958 Christmas rescue of the house with "no heat" was resolved very quickly. Preparing for the job took longer than the job itself.

There was a family Christmas party being held at the home of one of Poppy's customers. It was much like the one we left, only more festive. Aunts, uncles, and cousins had gathered at their grandparent's home. Gene and I went on the "no heat" call more for companionship than anything. Poppy investigated the problem and discovered that one of the cousins had dropped a crayon on the furnace. The crayon melted and the hole that supplied the gas was covered with crayon wax. Once the wax was removed, the furnace fired up. Problem solved.

We returned quickly to our gathering and the evening concluded much as it had started – missing Grandma.

I don't know how Poppy got his name, but all of the cousins called him that. When I spoke with my friends I referred to my mom's parents as Grandma and Grandpa Barner. Within the family, his grandchildren called him Poppy. If Gene or I were feeling frisky, we just called him Pop.

News of Grandma's passing was a horrible thing for our immediate family, however, single women saw an opportunity. While I don't know how long he waited before he "started dating" again, I do remember that during the Christmas season of 1959, Poppy received sixteen different shirts from sixteen different women. He was a sixty-year-old man with many suitors hoping to win his heart. He was successful, charming, fun-loving and alone. Many of the women were customers of Barner Heating hoping to become a co-owner. None did.

In the spring of 1960 we gathered for somebody's birthday without Poppy. He was visiting a friend, Virginia Wand Gibbs. The adult conversation centered on Virginia and her relationship with

Poppy. This was one of those, "if you stay quiet in the room," you can listen conversations.

Virginia was not new to our family. Her parents, the Wands, served as the landlords for Poppy's mom, "Old Granny Barner" in Bowling Green, Kentucky for several years. We met the Wand family during our visits to Kentucky. The extended families of the Wands and Barners became good friends.

Virginia was a widow of many years. Poppy started seeing her as a "female friend" to accompany him to social gatherings. It appeared that their relationship was becoming more serious and not everyone in the family was happy about it. The brief exchange about someone replacing their mother ended when Uncle Harry Barner said, "She was my mother too. I love her, but she's not here anymore. My dad is. He is a young man, and if Virginia makes him happy, I want him to be happy."

In August of 1960 Harrison Barner and Virginia Wand Gibbs married. I had a new Grandma and Grandpa Barner. I was thirteen years old. I liked her from the moment I met her. That changed briefly when I heard a group of adults discussing children. She had two. My new Aunt Ann, and her brother, Don, were great additions to our family.

At some point in the discussion she said, "I think that children should be seen but not heard." It was a quick off the cuff statement made in a casual conversation. I didn't like it. I wanted to be listened to. While I never forgot the statement, I learned to love her and accept her as my grandmother. She was kind to everyone, and as Poppy aged she became very protective of him.

They lived in the house on Troester for several years. After Poppy retired they moved to New Port Richey, Florida. Family gatherings moved as well. Thanksgiving dinner rotated among the siblings and birthdays were hosted by the celebrating parents. We continued to eat our way through our traditions, but life was never really the same after Margaret passed.

. . .

*I never saw Poppy get mad or raise his voice.* I expect that he did - don't we all - but I never witnessed it. His sons-in-law respected him. Tony, Harry, Don and Joe were not afraid to tease him, and they loved him like a father.

*He was a storyteller.* He may have exaggerated a little, but when he spoke, people listened. He told stories about his life and the people who touched it.

*Poppy loved ice cream.* He ate it almost every night. With Margaret it was primarily vanilla with Hersey's Chocolate Syrup. Virginia added new temptations like peach and butter pecan.

*He listened before he spoke.* He offered advice to those who sought it but thought before he answered. His words were concise. He gave it to you straight. If he thought you were out of line, he told you so. He didn't chastise but encouraged you to think it through.

*Poppy was playful.* After I married Ruth, he saw her bare feet and marveled at the length and strength of her toes. She won every toe wrestling contest, and he watched in amazement as she defeated (no pun intended) anyone who chose to challenge her.

*He was a teacher.* I shaved for the first time when I was sixteen. I had a dark mustache that I wanted to get rid of. He asked what type of razor I used "straight or safety."

"Straight." (I thought electric razors were safety razors.)

He chuckled. "No, you use a safety razor. You change the blades on a safety razor and use a leather strap to sharpen a straight razor. You change the blades on yours…right?

"Yes."

"How often do you change the blade?"

"I haven't."

He chuckled again.

*He taught me the meaning of hard work.* The summer that I got my driver's license, I worked with him for three weeks. We spent most of the time "cleaning" furnaces. This was a time when many coal-fired furnaces were still in use. Most gas furnaces were retrofitted from coal-burning.

Cleaning a gas furnace required the removal of a whatchamacallit and the clearing of the gas flow line. He taught me how to "remove, clear and replace" the whatchamacallit.

Cleaning a coal-fired furnace took more time and was much dirtier. I reached through the furnace door with large metal brushes and scraped soot off of the inside of the furnace wall. Once that was done, I stuck my head into the furnace door, put my hands in the door used to remove coal ash, and sucked up the dirt with a large, industrial "shop vac."

It was a dirty job. I ended each day by washing my hair multiple times to get rid of the soot.

*Poppy taught me the value associated with being the boss.* Once I had mastered both furnace cleaning techniques, I was allowed to clean the furnaces on my own while he drank coffee and ate pie with the lady of the house. Working with him was one of the reasons that I chose to seek a job that required me to use my brain rather than my back.

## Chapter 26

## AKA Woody

My cousin, Gene, is four years older than me. He's the oldest of twelve cousins. I'm number two and his sister, Ruth Ann, falls third on the list. His given name is Harry Eugene, but most of his friends call him Woody. I believe his mom and dad called him Gene (followed by our extended family) because we already had two Harrys and a Harrison in the clan.

The origin of Woody is a chicken or the egg conundrum for me. Gene has a tattoo of Woody Woodpecker. I don't know if people called him Woody because of the tattoo or if he got the tattoo because his friends called him Woody. I expect the former because he looks nothing like Woody Woodpecker.

I have dozens of stories about Gene, but I'll begin with one most pressing. Gene and Ruth Ann celebrate birthdays a few days apart in late November. Our family Thanksgiving dinners often included a celebration of these two birthdays. This is the Thanksgiving 2017 weekend, so I expect you are starting to see the connection.

One summer, I believe the summer of 1955, Gene's mom, my Aunt Ruth, was very ill. My Uncle Harry worked long hours. The care of his mother fell upon eleven-year-old Gene. He prepared food, administered medication, cleaned the house, did laundry, helped his mom dress and keep herself clean, while all the other kids his age were out playing ball, riding their bikes and just being kids.

Ruth Ann spent much of that summer at our house. She had a kid type summer in a neighboring town. My mom traveled to help her sister after my dad got home from work. He worked long hours too. The trips to help ran late into the evening and were taken every day. My mom and Gene became a care giving team. While Mom and Gene had a strong bond prior to that summer, I know it grew stronger because of their care giving duties. That bond remained strong throughout the remainder of my mother's life.

I don't actually remember all of the details of that summer. My mom talked about it more than once over her lifetime and the story remained the same. She felt bad for Gene because he was thrust into growing up faster than most. She also told me he was more like a son to her than a nephew. I expect that was a result of their shared duties and love of my aunt.

Over the years, Gene has continued his care giving ways. He is always around when anyone needs any help. Moving, fixing, just lending an extra set of hands, he's done it all. When my parents were still alive, he was a dependable "go to" guy. When my father passed, he became even more important to my mother. While I was around to help, I lived two hours away. Gene lived closer and was more immediately available. Car issues, running toilets, or a flooding basement, Gene stepped up.

Moving forward I'll have more Gene stories to share, but no matter how many I may post, the most important one is this one because it tells the tale of the birth of my mother's second son.

## Chapter 27

## Two Bits from My Past

I spent the winter in Florida. During my time there, I had the opportunity to meet with my cousin, Gene, on a couple of occasions. He has a Florida home too. If you are an avid reader of my blog, you know that Gene is AKA Woody. We did a lot of reminiscing. Here are a couple of stories from our childhood. While I don't wish for these to be written on my tombstone, I hope you can handle the truth and don't think less of either of us because of these revelations.

In no particular order of significance, I give you:

**The Great Cat Caper**

My Grandma Barner, my mom's mom, died at the young age of fifty-nine. My grandfather became a widower at fifty-nine. After an appropriate time for grieving, Grandpa Barner started dating and about three years later, he remarried. He married Virginia who had been a family friend for many years. Virginia's parents lived in Bowling Green, Kentucky. Her parents had a one-bedroom apartment in their home that they rented to my Grandpa Barner's mother for several years. That's the key reason that the two families knew each other.

I was thirteen and Gene was seventeen when Harrison and Virginia married. One day shortly after the wedding, we were at my grandparents' house when my mom and Gene's mom, my Aunt Ruth, decided to play a trick on my grandfather and his new bride. They short-sheeted the wedding bed. I never understood the thrill of short-sheeting someone's bed, but they thought it was great fun.

My Aunt Ruth decided to spice things up a bit, so she rolled peanut butter into little balls and put the peanut butter balls into my grandpa's underwear. The idea was to—well, you get the idea. Peanut butter balls in your underwear could be cause for a surprise.

Gene and I watched and decided that we should develop a surprise of our own. We didn't know what we were going to do, but we were determined to join in the fun. We got into Gene's car and started to drive the alleys of Detroit looking for an inspiration. It didn't take long to discover our surprise and develop a plan. We found a large white Angora cat tied to a post in a backyard. Gene kept the car running. I opened the gate to the yard, untied the cat, grabbed it and jumped into the car. Gene drove off.

When we got back to the house we snuck into our grandparents' bedroom, tied the cat under the bed, and left just enough rope so the cat could crawl around under the bed without exposing itself. Pure genius.

While we weren't around to witness the big surprise, when my grandparents went to bed that night the cat began to meow. I don't know that they identified the source of the meowing immediately, but I do know that they did eventually. The next day we received a telephone call and returned to the house to fetch the cat. We returned to the scene of the crime, replaced the cat, and the caper was over.

I know the two of us have continued to celebrate the great cat caper long after the sheets were returned to their normal length and the last peanut butter ball had been discovered.

### Speaking of Bathrooms

This next tale is a bit embarrassing. But it's the truth.

Our extended family had a lot of gatherings. We celebrated everything. Every time someone had a birthday, we got together for cake and ice cream. While preparing for a trip to my Aunt Ruth and Uncle Harry's (Gene's parents) for somebody's something, I discovered that I didn't have any clean underwear. I told my mom, and she gave me a pair of hers to wear. I was about five, and in the time it takes to say "holy cow" I became America's youngest cross-dresser. I don't remember much about my new wears, and perhaps I wouldn't have remembered anything at all if it weren't for my cousin, Gene.

I didn't question my mom. Looking back, I could have just dressed commando style that day, or perhaps flipped a pair of my about-to-be-laundered drawers and worn them inside out. But I didn't. I did as I was told.

After arriving at my aunt and uncle's house, I needed to go to the bathroom. I had to go "number two" which required sitting down on the toilet.

Nine-year-old Gene was occupying the bathroom, but he invited me to join him. As he was washing his hands and preparing to depart, I dropped my pants and took a seat. (We were close cousins and about to get closer.) He noted that I was wearing pink underwear and asked where I got them. I told him the story of my laundry dilemma and my mom's directive to put on a pair of hers. He started to laugh. About the time he started laughing, his dad, my Uncle

Harry, knocked on the door. Seems he had to use the bathroom too. Gene invited him in. Our bathroom crowd was getting bigger as each moment passed.

My uncle had poor eyesight and wore thick glasses to help him see. He may not even have noticed the pink panties if Gene hadn't pointed them out. But he did. So, we had a five-year old sitting on the toilet wearing a pair of his mother's underwear, his nine-year old cousin laughing at his miss-fortune, and the cousin's thirty-something dad joining in the laugh fest at the five-year old's expense.

Throughout the remainder of my life, I have made sure that no one saw my underwear unless I deemed it appropriate. I also took a private vow that I would never wear ladies' underwear again. So far so good.

## Chapter 28

## Born to Be Wild

If Mom were still alive, she would have turned 101 last Monday. While she had three children, Sharron, Jackie, and me, she often told me that my cousin, Gene, was more like a son than a nephew. He was the oldest cousin from the Barner clan and the "go-to" man in the family. He assisted anyone who needed help without seeking compensation for his efforts. Other family members expected to be paid when lending a hand. Not Gene.

As soon as he could drive, he bought a car. He bought and sold cars so often that my Grandpa Barner thought the "pink slips," car registrations, passed one another in the mail. He bought and sold faster than the state could register them.

Later, he started riding motorcycles. Like his cars, he had several different rides. One day while our family was visiting him, he was showing us his latest "bike," a Honda Superhawk. My dad took an interest in the bike and asked Gene if he could take it for a ride. "Sure. Have you ever driven one?"

"No, but how hard can it be?"

Gene showed him how the kick start worked and he was off. We watched from the rear as he weaved his way down Chippewa Street in Mt. Clemens, narrowly missing the curbs on both sides. We were starting to wonder how the ride went when we looked down the street and saw him pushing the bike home. He had stopped at a stop sign and the engine had cut out. He tried to kick start it, but he couldn't get it going. After several failed attempts, he pushed it the final five blocks.

By the time my mom had reached her nineties, Gene had moved on to three-wheel motorcycles called trikes. They're easier for older riders to handle. We all met for lunch one day, and Gene had ridden his trike. Mom was always up for an adventure, so she accepted his offer to go for a ride. She sported his extra helmet, and they took off down Hall Road not far from the Lakeside Mall. I wish I could have seen the reaction of those who saw this dynamic duo.

# Chapter 29

## Have You Stayed Here Before?

I walked up to the counter and the attractive young attendant countered my, "I have a reservation." with "Have you stayed here before?" I had.

Another time, another place, I might have thought that this was a pickup line, but I'm too old to be picked up. The last time I stayed at the Chesterfield Hampton Inn was April 27, 2014. I booked four rooms for my family. We were there for my mother's funeral. This time I was checking in for my cousin Gene's. Staying in this hotel is becoming an unwelcome habit.

I've delayed writing this blog because it's tough. I'm losing too many people I care about. You expect to lose your parents one day, but when your peers start passing, you address your own mortality as well. I've got things to do and repeated stays at the Hampton Inn is not on the list.

I've written about Gene several times since beginning my blog. He and his first wife, Sandy, shared thirty-nine years and raised two sons. After Sandy passed, he was lucky to find Lauren to share his remaining years.

Speaking in public has been a part of my life for fifty years. Most of the time, I enjoy it. As I've gotten older, I get emotional when I speak about things that I feel passionate about or people I love.

When the minister asked for those present to share memories of Gene at today's service, I knew I couldn't do it. I have lots to say, lots to share, but not on this day. Luckily, my youngest sister, Jackie, was able to speak. Her words were simple, but heartfelt. She, like everyone present, loved Gene and her words hit home for everyone.

Take a look.

*Gene is my older cousin by ten years, and I felt like he was my brother from another mother. He was probably the coolest guy I knew. I never knew anyone other than Gene, and Fonzie, who kept their cigarettes rolled in the sleeve of their t-shirt.*

*He brought a cool girl to a family picnic, and she had cool leather pants. When Sandy and Gene married and had the boys, she wasn't cool anymore. She was a mother. He was still cool, but he had a huge heart.*

*He would help anyone. I remember this cool guy carrying his grandma Mac who had lost a leg. He helped our Grandpa Barner when he was grieving the loss of our grandmother.*

*Over the years, he has fixed my cars, roofed my garage, babysat my children, supported me, helped our parents, teased me and loved me. And I loved him. He loved his family and our extended family, and we all loved him.*

*Gene could be braggadocios, but not intentionally, and in my opinion only about two things, his sons and grandsons. He was proud of all and shared that with me on many occasions.*

*This past St. Patrick's Day, I reminded Gene and Lauren of the first time I heard about Lauren. It was probably twelve years ago on St. Patrick's Day. I had called him to see what he was doing, and he said he was going out for corned beef and cabbage.*

*I said, "With who?"*

*He said, "Lauren."*

*And of course, I wanted to know who this Lauren was.*
*"It's not a date."*
*"Are you paying the bill?"*
*"Yes."*
*"Then it's a date, and she will think it's a date."*

*I made it a point to endear myself to Lauren. I wanted to know if this sweet girl was worthy of his love and was she going to love him? She was, and she did. He was lucky to have two good women who loved him, and they were lucky too. We were all lucky.*

*I hope when I leave this world I find him, and the first place I'm going to look is with the cool kids.*

# Chapter 30

# James A. Marvin

I met Jim Marvin about 30 years ago at a poker game. I was invited to sub with a group that he belonged to. I liked him right away. Eventually, I became a member of the group and while playing several hundred hands of cards, we became good friends. The group took turns hosting the game and I met Jim's wife, Diane, when we played at their house. I liked her too. Ruth met Jim when it was my turn to host a game. She eventually met Diane and over time the four of us shared a special bond.

We traveled, shared our families with each other, and have grown through our "maturing years" together.

I have considered Jim my best friend for the past two dozen years. He and I shared stories of our lives, sought each other's counsel, dreamed and planned together, and lived a good life.

He was a good man who thought of others before himself. He willingly shared his time, advice, and wealth. He gave the gift of himself and was a friend to anyone who needed one. He volunteered. He made a difference. Most importantly, he did it without thought of personal gain or accolades.

Jim was a private man. After all the years of sharing time, I have few pictures of him. While others post each moment of their life on social media, Jim was never tempted. He kept most of his thoughts to himself but would share his opinion when asked. He never insisted that you subscribe to his train of thought but made it clear where he stood.

We discussed our children and grandchildren. He was proud of Tracy and Michael, their accomplishments, and the lives that they created for themselves. The only time that I heard Jim lament was when Michael decided to move out of state. I told him that I felt the same when my daughter, Elizabeth, and son, Michael, moved away. And then I reminded him, "We can't raise our children to be independent and then feel sorry for ourselves when they are." He reluctantly agreed.

When Jim served on the Hudson Education Foundation Board, he met a girl that he thought deserved more help than the foundation could offer. Without her knowledge, he privately sponsored her education and was proud of the woman that she has become.

When we were building a new sports complex in Britton, we drove to see the project one Sunday afternoon. Jim was particularly fond of baseball and inquired how much the new dugouts were projected to cost. Within the week, the Britton Education Foundation received a check from Jim and Diane to pay for the dugouts.

When my kids came to visit us in The Villages, he drove 30 miles one-way to buy donuts from a special shop that he valued so that he could share his treasure with my children and grandchildren.

He provided the scholarship, paid for the dugouts, and drove to buy donuts because it was important to share what he had with others.

Jim, Diane, Ruth, and I have visited our share of casinos and engaged in several games of chance. Jim may be the only man I know that won more than he lost. When we discussed the winning and the losing, we both agreed that we preferred to win rather than lose, however, neither of us had plans for any money that we might win.

We really didn't care how it might be spent. Having more than you had when started was the only goal. Money was merely the way we kept score.

Of all the things we discussed, including lost loved ones, we never discussed our own mortality. We never shared our beliefs about what might happen after we are gone. While we both planned for the financial repercussions and shared those plans, we never discussed being gone.

Now he's gone and he took a piece of me with him. But more importantly, he left a piece of himself with me. I'll never forget our friendship and how, over time, we became more like brothers than friends and that's how I'll remember Jim.

Last November, I started writing a blog. My goal is to write true stories for my grandchildren. A legacy of sorts for them. Jim read my stories and commented on them from time to time. Always in person. Never on-line.

Jim, Diane, Ruth, and I traveled to Biloxi, Mississippi last winter and one morning during breakfast, a woman came up to our table and asked if I remembered her. I did.

The following week, I posted a story called, "Do You Remember Me?" A few days later, Jim spoke to me about the story and commented that he particularly liked a couple of lines. They read as follows:

For most of us being remembered means that we have had purpose. That while we are here, we've made a difference. We want someone to remember and share our story.

While the private side of Jim may not wish the notoriety, I plan to write more about him for as long as I am able. His story is too special to go unshared.

# Chapter 31

# The Patsy

Our neighborhood was full of young families with children. By the time kids stopped being born, the head counts went something like this:

1. Tebo (that's us) 3
2. Ruff (left side of us) 4 (later replaced by the Benedicts with 3)
3. Graham (across from Ruff) 2 (underachievers)
4. Coatta (right side of Graham) 6 (There is about a 20-year spread between number 1 and number 6)
5. Mattson (left side of Graham and across from us) 4
6. Conti (down on the corner by the park) 3
7. Prested (right side of us) 27

There were other families with children too, but these are the kids I grew up knowing and playing with. Mitch came from around the block and joined us almost every day. When Mitch's younger brother Jimmy got older, he joined us too. We played in back yards (Graham's had a swing set), the street, (tennis and baseball with a tennis ball), driveways (tennis ball hockey), assorted games of frozen tag/poison tag, hide and seek, and the ever popular, politically insensitive, "cowboys and Indians." All good stuff until the porch light came on and you had to go in. (Families could only afford one car so the empty street was part of our play yard.)

The highlight of the street took place in the summer. When summer storms rolled through, the storm sewer couldn't handle the rain and the street flooded. We had our own swimming pool. When the rain let up, we just ran around in our bathing suits to cool down.

We also had a park at the end of the street where, when we got older, the guys all played baseball. One day, on the way home from one of our baseball games, Bill Graham and I got into an argument. The argument grew as we walked down the street, and ultimately, came to blows. I don't remember the argument, but I remember the blows. It's the only time in my life that I got into a real, honest to goodness, knockdown, drag out, toe-to-toe boxing match. It was our version of the Gillette Blue Blade Friday Night Fights on a Wednesday afternoon.

Bill struck the first blow by slapping me with his baseball glove. That blow led to some basic pushing and shoving. We started exchanging punches and the full-out battle began. At one point, Bill ran across the street towards his house. We ended up between his house and the Mattson's. I pushed him up against the fence a couple of times and yelled at him repeatedly to take off his glasses. He wouldn't. I grew tired of my frustration and blasted him in the face, breaking his glasses and enraging the bull. We exchanged a series of punches. Half of Bill's glasses had fallen to the ground and the other half remained on his face.

The fight ended when we both got tired. He was mad because of his broken glasses. I was mad because he hadn't taken them off. By the time the fight was over, we were both mad because we didn't know what we were fighting about. Bill and I were like most boys. When the fight was over, we went back to being friends.

I thought my parents would be mad about the broken glasses,

but they weren't. Bill was supposed to get new glasses, so the broken ones just expedited the process. Lucky me.

Before the summer was over "lucky me" turned into "what the heck me." Bill got his new glasses as planned, but several weeks later they were broken. I wasn't involved. I really can't say how or why they were broken, but one afternoon my mom called me aside to tell me that a man was coming to our house. "When the man arrives, you need to tell him that you broke Bill's glasses."

"You mean when we had the fight earlier this summer?"

"No, you need to tell him that you broke them now."

I didn't understand. I didn't break them now.

"The man is from our insurance company, and you need to tell him that you broke Bill's glasses. You're not in trouble, but the man needs to know that you broke the glasses, so he'll buy Bill some new ones."

When the insurance man came, I did as mom directed. I was an eleven-year-old crying liar. I sobbed and sobbed as I retold the tale of the fight and how I had broken the glasses. And although the insurance man told me everything would be alright, I didn't feel that way.

Somewhere around the time I turned 45 or 46, I figured all of this out. We committed an insurance scam so Bill could get new glasses. Our insurance company would have paid for Bill's glasses when I broke them during the fight. He didn't need new glasses then because his parents had already bought him new ones. Later, when he did need new glasses, I was directed to tell a false truth so he could get them. My mother felt I should take the blame so everything would be OK. Bill would have new glasses. I had broken his, even if I hadn't broken the ones I was directed to claim I broke. I was **The Patsy**.

All the homes in our neighborhood had two doors. The front door was where most kids went to call upon their friends. For example, if I wanted Bill to come out to play, I would stand on his front porch and call his name repeatedly until someone answered.

"Billeeeeey!!! Billeeeeey!!! Billeeeeey!!!" Eventually, someone would answer the door.

The side door was the child door. All the kids entered and exited through this door. You stepped onto a "landing" when you entered. You either went up two steps to the kitchen or down a dozen to the basement. You entered through a double-door system. The first door was a screen, or glass door, depending on the season. The screen door was installed during spring, summer and fall. The glass door was for winter. Fathers were in charge of installing and replacing the screen or glass insert from season to season. The wooden doors were white unless the owner decided to paint them a different color.

One summer day, somebody took crayons and drew pictures all over our next-door neighbors, The Prested's, child door. When Mrs. Prested (AKA Gert) discovered the vandalized door, she asked several of her twenty-seven children who was responsible for the "coloring." The twenty-seven children all came forward with the same story. "Robbie did it."

I'm here to tell you that Robbie didn't do it. I'm Robbie. I don't know who did it, but I know I didn't.

Mrs. Prested came over to my house to tell my mother about the "coloring" on the door. I wasn't around during the trial, but when I did appear the judges (my mom and Mrs. Prested) and the witnesses (the twenty-seven Prested kids) determined I was guilty. While I declared my innocence, my mom wouldn't listen. My sentence was to wash the door, remove all the "coloring," and then report to my room for the rest of the day. I was punished for something I didn't do. The twenty-seven members of the "liar, liar, pants on fire" collective colluded to convict me. Once again, I was **The Patsy**.

## Chapter 32

## The Underachiever

The importance of hard work was instilled upon me by my parents. My mom graduated from high school but my dad only attended school through the eighth grade. That was normal for many kids born in the late teens and twenties. They wanted more for my two sisters and me. They encouraged me to work hard in school which by most accounts, including my grade point average, fell on deaf ears. I never "studied hard" or got great grades. I did all of my required work and achieved what I achieved by doing the minimum. I was bright. Capable of doing more. But I preferred to just get by. My teachers and my mom saw "my potential" and discussed it with me at great length. "If you only apply yourself, you'll achieve great things." I remember telling my mom one day, "I don't want my friends to think I'm too smart." Mission accomplished. They didn't.

I was in the Cub Scouts and Boy Scouts. Being involved in scouting provided me with another way to learn – through experience. Even there I did my best to avoid things that required "study." One time we put on a play that involved pirates attacking and boarding a sailing ship. The scout leader wanted me to play the part of the captain of the ship that was being attacked. The opening scene had the captain speaking to his first mate about their journey. The role required memorizing lines that would set the stage for the entire play and make me "the star." I didn't want to have anything to do with it. The scout leader spoke to my mom and she encouraged me to take on the role. No dice. I wanted to be one of the pirates that attacked and boarded the ship. None of the pirates had any lines to memorize and I preferred that option.

When I was in the fourth grade the scouts put on a minstrel show. (Try doing that today.) I remember that this took place while I was in the fourth grade because I broke my ankle while trick or treating on Halloween. I ended up in a walking cast following the break and appeared on stage in my cast. I had agreed to serve as the "only white face" in the "black face" minstrel show. I served as the Interlocutor. The Interlocutor was the "straight man" and the key figure in the variety show. I agreed because they allowed me to have the script at my feet for reference.

I still remember one exchange that went like this.

"Mr. Interlocutor, did you ever notice Mr. Martin's big feet."

"Well, yes. Now that you mention it, Mr. Martin's feet are rather large."

"Large! Large!! That man's feet are magnanimous!!!"

When I was older, I moved up to Boy Scouts. I loved the Boy Scouts. We went camping, earned merit badges, and marched to cool rhyming chants. Fun stuff. We told ghost stories and jokes around a camp fire. Winter camping took place in bunk houses and summer camping required tents. My dad went winter camping one week-end with us. He did all of the cooking and most of the dish washing for our troop. That's the only time that I ever went camping with my dad. I can still see him cooking chili and washing out the big pot after the evening meal. I think that he acquired his skill in the kitchen while serving in the army.

My merit badges included: cooking, reading, camp fire making, and horsemanship. There were over a hundred opportunities to earn merit badges and I earned four. I took the path of least resistance and did what I had to do to earn the four, including eating "almost" raw chicken on the final test for my cooking merit badge. The camp fire making and cooking badges were earned through the same project. You had to build a fire in order to do the cooking. My big claim to fame was that I learned how to bridle and saddle a horse, and get him to walk, canter, and gallop.

The thing I enjoyed most about scouting was the "doing" part. I didn't want to study. I just wanted "to do."

Eventually, I did do just what I needed to do to move on. I was never in a place that I would truly call failure. My high school grade point average was 2.27, college undergrad 2.54, master's program 3.8 and Specialist degree 4.0. My success as a student was measured in numbers with decimal points. I expect that had my mom known of my gradual grade improvement she would have approved. She, and the teachers of my early years, would have seen me reach my potential.

The truth of the matter is I started "doing" things. The "doing" was driven by my desire to "do" more. As the "doing" increased so did my grades. I was engaged and found purpose. I expect that most of us who have found satisfaction in our life have done so by moving forward to accomplish our goals.

I joined organizations in college, took on leadership roles, and loved the experience. When I became a teacher, I taught outside of the book, as a principal I strove to garner a staff that worked together to make learning exciting, and as a superintendent I worked to improve the culture so that everyone was proud of who they were and who they planned to become. There was always more "to do."

If you're lucky, you have things to accomplish, goals to achieve, things "to do" throughout your entire life. Things to get up for each morning and people to share your accomplishments. As for me, I plan to keep on "doing" – to keep on keepin on.

# Chapter 33

# Thank You, Ken

I was twenty-two when I started teaching at Plainwell Junior High in the fall of 1969. I had a girlfriend who was still in college, and I drove a 1967 Mustang convertible. I lived in an apartment that cost $75.00 per person with my good friend, Mike. My first contract was for $6,900. I started a savings account and began to look for a house to buy. My take-home check was $149.00 every two weeks and there was more than one time when I had two or three uncashed checks in my wallet.

I taught two sections of seventh grade geography and the balance of my classes were seventh grade English. The name of our English text was "Roberts Linguistics." I wasn't a fan. My first-hour English students were all in the band and very bright. If it weren't for this first hour group of high achieving students, "Roberts Linguistics" and I would have never made it through the day. I learned as much from this group of bright kids as they did from me.

Two other teachers shared the responsibility for teaching geography. Jim and Ken were a couple of years older and had experience working for them. Ken and I shared a prep period, so we had several opportunities to discuss upcoming lessons and study units. Our big claim to fame was organizing the local observance of the first "Earth Day." The three of us did our best to work on common themes so that we could exchange teaching ideas. Being a rookie, I could use all the guidance I could garner.

A series of lessons that we taught dealt with religion and the various practices of groups throughout the world. The common technology of the day was the tried-and-true *filmstrip*. We had an entire series of filmstrips to assist us with our review of world religions. We had one set, so we had to coordinate this resource between the three of us. One morning, Ken asked me if I had reviewed the filmstrip regarding Christianity. I hadn't. He told me that I should review it prior to showing it in class as it referenced the circumcision of Jesus.

A day or two later, Ken told me he had used the filmstrip and a question arose from one of the students. The student had asked, "What does circumcision mean?"

"What did you say? How did you answer the question?"

"The removal of the foreskin from the penis."

"Did they ask anything else?"

"No. They accepted my explanation and we moved on. I just want you to be prepared."

And so, I was. My geography classes met the last two hours of the day. I planned to use the filmstrip the following day. When the next day rolled around, I was ready. Ken had armed me with a "heads up." As I advanced through the filmstrip, right on cue, a voice came from the darkened room.

"Mr. Tebo."

"Yes."

"What does circumcision mean?"

I was ready. "Circumcision is the removal of the foreskin from the penis." Asked and answered.

We moved on and class went well. I was very happy that Ken had provided the "heads up."

The next hour class arrived, and I was moving through the

filmstrip aided lesson, when right on cue a voice came out of the darkness, "Mr. Tebo."

"Yes, Henry." I recognized the voice as belonging to a student, Henry, who had moved from Arkansas to Plainwell during the summer. He was new to our school and had a very distinctive southern accent. In addition to being from the South, he was a bit mischievous.

"What does circumcision mean?" Thanks to Ken this was not going to be a problem.

"Circumcision is the removal of the foreskin from the penis." Once again, asked and answered.

As I moved on to the next frame in the filmstrip, the voice came once again.

"Mr. Tebo."

"Yes, Henry."

"What's a penis?"

Now this was something I hadn't considered. Ken hadn't mentioned it, but here it was. My nimble brain needed to think quickly. I knew Henry was putting me on. He was testing the young teacher and thought he had me stumped. All I could muster was, "Henry, if you're serious, stay after class and we'll talk about it."

He didn't stay.

Most of the junior high teachers had a homeroom. My group was 7-D (7th grade, fourth group). We had a series of activities organized around homerooms. One of the big competitions was a basketball tournament. There was a boys' tournament and a girls' tournament. (Separate but equal) I was fortunate to have a pretty good group of girls. One of the girls, Valarie, could do it all – shoot, dribble, rebound, pass and she was lightning fast. Coaching basketball was not my strong suit, but I enjoyed working with the kids and had a good time.

During one exciting, close game, I called time out so that we could set up a play. I don't remember the play, and I wouldn't have remembered any of the tournament if it weren't for Ken. As the timeout ended, I sent the girls back onto the court, and as I did, I patted Valarie on the butt. I probably said something like, "Get in there and make the shot."

I don't know if it was later that day, or the next morning during our planning hour, Ken pointed out the error of my ways. "Bob, you can't be patting girls on the butt." I didn't know what he was talking about. He recounted my steps during the timeout, and sure enough, I did pat Valarie on the butt. I was caught up in the excitement of the game and gave her a pat of encouragement, which if taken in the wrong context, could have been seen as being sexual. It wasn't, but Ken was right, I shouldn't have. I kept my hands in my pockets throughout the rest of the tournament.

Ken was an advocate for making sure he understood a student's question before he attempted to answer it. Ken wanted to provide accurate information, but he needed to understand the question to accomplish his goal.

I thought this was good practice, and I tried following that path myself. Honesty and frankness should serve me well.

One day I took my geography class to the library to conduct research for a project that they were developing. While the kids did their work, I sat on the edge of one of the library tables so everyone could see me in case they needed to ask a question. I wanted to be available but not intrusive. I corrected papers while they moved freely around the library. Students came up often to seek my council. I was a multi-tasker, so I was able to keep correcting papers while answering their questions. This system worked very well until Ed asked a question that needed more thought.

"Mr. Tebo."

"Yes." (Still correcting papers)

"What does intercourse mean?"

I stopped correcting papers and thought –*remember honesty and frankness*. As I took a deep breath I thought, what *would Ken say?*

"Why do you ask?" (that's what I thought Ken would say)

"It's in this book and I don't understand."

"It is? Let me take a look."

I took the book and there it was in black and white. Intercourse. It's funny how your mind works. When I heard "intercourse" I was thinking sex. The black and white print in the book was referencing the *intercourse* between two countries. Thank God I followed Ken's clarifying approach.

"Ed, intercourse means the trade between these two countries. When they use the word, they're talking about the goods and services these two countries share."

"Thanks for your help, Mr. Tebo."

I said, "You're welcome." But what I was really thinking was, *thank you, Ken.*

# Chapter 34

# Jay and the Americans

Ruth and I attended a concert last Sunday night. It was a nostalgic walk through the history of Motown. We had a great trip. We knew all the songs and danced in our seats for the full hour and forty-five minutes.

Prior to the concert I stepped into the restroom to prepare for the event. As I looked into the mirror, I flashed back to a concert that I attended during my sophomore year at Western. I took a girl to see Jay and the Americans at the Read Field House. They were a hot group at the time. Jay Black was the lead singer, the second in a string of three Jays. He could hit the high notes that were required in many of their hits: *She Cried, Crying, Cara Mia, This Magic Moment, Come a Little Bit Closer,* and *Only in America.*

I would have loved the concert if I could have given my full attention to the music, but I couldn't. I'd like to say that I devoted my time to my date, but I didn't. If I could remember her name I'd share it, but I don't. I went out with her only once. She was nice enough, and I expect that she would have said, "yes," if I'd asked, but I didn't.

We had assigned bleacher seats. We were in the middle of a row with about 15-20 people seated to both our left and right. We settled in, and I was looking forward to hearing the group sing. They opened with "Only in America," a great song. Within the first stanza or two, my gut started to rumble. I had to fart but I couldn't, or rather, I wouldn't. I couldn't be sure if the expulsion would be smooth or deadly. I couldn't risk offending anyone, so I sat in silence, clenched my cheeks, and wallowed in misery.

Perhaps you've been there yourself.

In any case, I sat and considered my options. If I attempted to get up and excuse myself to use the restroom, I'd be butt-to-face with some unsuspecting coed or frat boy. I didn't want to offend either, so I just sat. I was afraid that one false move would lead to an ill-timed, smelly disaster. I hoped that if I got up, I could struggle by, but I chose to suffer in silence.

I believe that my clenched teeth may have looked like I was smiling. I hope so. There wasn't a lot of conversation because people were engrossed in the music. I was thankful for that. Each time the group transitioned from one song to the next, I could hear my gut rumble. I hoped that no one else could.

The concert lasted about 100 continuous hours. There were no breaks. No intermissions.

When it was time to leave, I made sure that everyone around me was standing. I double clenched and rose slowly. I timed each careful step with the noise of the crowd. I could probably avoid the noise that a fart might make, but you can never be sure of the aroma. Caution guided my every move.

We headed out to the parking lot. The buildup was so great that I was sure that the noise would be deafening. I couldn't risk even the most minor release. I walked my date to the passenger side, opened the door for her, and once she was settled, I moved to the rear of the car. I opened the trunk and let her rip. I used the noise from the squeaking trunk as a diversion. Leaves fell from the trees.

Thankfully a gentle breeze helped disperse the gas. I felt sorry for those who might be downwind, but by the time the gas reached anyone else, it could have come from anywhere. It took an eternity to clear my pipes, and I waited a bit longer to ensure that no lingering signs remained in my slacks. Once I was confident that all was clear, I got in the car. I made some lame excuse about opening the trunk, and we were on our way.

The rest of the evening was uneventful. We stopped for something to eat, went to the student union to shoot pool, and eventually I took her back to the dorm. It was the weekend so our date ended just prior to 1:00 a.m. We said our goodbyes, agreed that we should go out again sometime, but we didn't.

The memory of that night, and what might have happened, still haunts me. That's why for the past fifty plus years, I stop in the restroom before attending any concert. You never know when you might want to dance in your seat like we did last Sunday.

## Chapter 35

## Another Poker Tale

I started playing poker with a new group of guys in The Villages about six weeks ago. There's a guy from Virginia, one from Pennsylvania, another from Maryland, and three from New York. Nobody drinks alcohol. They're focused on the cards. They take fifty cents from each pot until they reach twenty-five dollars (fifty hands), and one of the guys buys snacks, bottled water, and new playing cards for the group with the money.

They play split pot games with unusual names and unique rules: The Clock 7-Low, The Clock with Runs, Rufus's Game (named after a deceased friend named Rufus), Fifty-Two, Columns, Wagon Train, Pyramid, Christmas Tree, The Good the Bad and the Ugly. The list seems endless. I've never played or heard of them before. They play at least twice a week and deal as fast as they can. I've learned several new games and stirred up some old memories.

I played for several years with a group from Hillsdale and the surrounding area. We were good friends gathered around a poker table every other week. I started as a substitute with the group, and ultimately, worked my way in as a full-time participant. That's how I met my friend, Jim. We played poker together and discovered we had a similar outlook on life.

We played exactly seventy hands each time we met. We took a dollar from every pot. When we had seventy dollars, the night was over. We saved the seventy dollars until we had several hundred and then planned a gambling trip to Las Vegas or Atlantic City. If we played every two weeks as planned, we'd have a total of $1,820 at the end of the year. We either purchased tickets for the trip or divided the money as our "stake" once we arrived at the gambling site.

One time we used the money to purchase junket tickets to Atlantic City. This was a designated flight filled with people who wished to gamble. There were one hundred and six people on board. We were asked by the flight attendants if we'd like to place our first wager during the flight. They explained that if everyone put up $5.00, they would hold a drawing and award half the money to two people. With one hundred and six people on board, we'd have two pots of $265. Everyone bought in. Our crew of five agreed to split the $265 equally. Each of us would receive $53.00 if one of us won. The two winners were determined by a random seat draw. Each of us wrote our seat number on the five-dollar bill we put in the pot.

The drawing was held just before we began our descent into Atlantic City. My five-dollar bill was one of the winners. A flight attendant gave me a brown paper bag with fifty-three five-dollar bills. We were ahead before we even touched down.

Once we landed, I took my bag of five-dollar bills on the shuttle to the casino. During the drive, the five of us decided to try to parlay our collective stash into an even greater win. We'd place several wagers on a variety of games. We'd bet on blackjack, play a hand of pai gow poker, a hand of baccarat, shoot craps, put some money down on the "Big Wheel" and try our luck on the roulette wheel. Since my five-dollar bill had been drawn, I was designated to make all the bets.

We went to the casino cage to convert the five-dollar bills into larger currency. After making the conversion, we headed to the tables. We started with a hand of blackjack. I caught two eights against the dealer's six, split them, doubled one when I drew a two and won both bets. After that we went over to the dice table, and ultimately, moved through all the games. I won each one. We decided to press our luck again and did the same tour. I placed all the bets and never lost. After round two was complete, we divided the cash five ways. I had turned my five-dollar bill into $265 on board the plane and proceeded to parlay the $265 into $1,050. We each had $210.00 to play with, and we were just getting started.

The five of us split up. Three headed to the craps table, while Jim and I went off to play blackjack. After sizing up several tables, we decided to sit at a table with a $25.00 minimum bet. It was empty, so we'd had the table to ourselves. As we bought in, Jim needed to use the restroom and asked the dealer to save a place for him. The dealer replied, "I'll save the place, but this table has a no mid-shoe rule. You won't be able to buy in until the next shoe."

Then I asked, "Can I play two spots and have him take one of the spots when he returns?"

"Yes, but you have to play $50.00 on each spot if you play two.

I wanted Jim to be able to join in right away, so I said, "Ok." I bought in with my $210.00 stake and hoped for the best.

I'm not sure how long he was gone, but while Jim was in the restroom, I went on a roll. I won hand after hand, and if one of the two lost, the second won. By the time he sat down to buy in, I was up over $1,000 more. It was unbelievable. Jim bought in, and I dropped to just one hand. We finished the shoe and played one more. We won a few and lost a few. There was no run, just a lot of pushing chips back and forth. Our run of good luck stopped.

When I cashed out from the table, I put an orange chip ($1,000) in my pocket and vowed not to touch it until we were headed home. I looked at my watch and noted we had cashed in my bag of five-dollar bills about an hour earlier. I was way up, and my good fortune all started with a $5.00 lucky seat drawing on the airplane.

## Chapter 36

## Like You Mean It

There's a saying... hindsight is 20/20. The expression comes from the way people describe good vision. A person with normal, good vision has 20/20 sight. Hindsight is an understanding of a past event. Looking back makes things look clearer. I don't know who coined the phrase, but it's been around as long as I can remember.

The year 2020 was full of trouble. If there were ever a year people wished was over, this was it. If you're reading this on "posting day," take a deep breath. You're almost there. I'm pretty sure very few people would like to relive 2020. With all its turmoil, I did learn a lesson I hope to keep for the rest of my days.

A couple of weeks ago, while helping my granddaughter, Eva, with her golf game, I noticed she did better when she swung more deliberately. She's played golf a few times over the years but not on a regular basis. She's got a nice, fluid, natural swing, and could be very good if she played more, but she hasn't. While at the driving range, she hit the turf time after time and became frustrated. That's a normal reaction for anyone. After each practice swing, she'd seek my advice. How did it look? Was she keeping her head down? Was she following through? What else should she do?

When we got to the first tee of the 130-yard par three, I told her to hit her four iron, and "swing like you mean it." She did. The ball hit the front of the green, rolled towards the back, and after two putts, she parred the hole. As the round progressed, she had successes and failures. The one constant was when she "hit it like she meant it," she did better.

I played in my first "men's day" of the season yesterday. As I walked to the first tee, I remembered the advice I offered Eva. "Swing like you mean it." I did, and I found success. I tried to play those words in my head with each shot and played my best round of the season. It's going to be my 'swing thought' from now on. Like Eva, I sometimes get discouraged when I hit a bad shot. I become tentative and don't give it my best. Having a positive swing thought helped me achieve success.

I think the idea has applications for activities other than golf. We should be living life like we mean it all the time. If it's worth doing, it's worth giving it our best shot. Being deliberate and intentional applies to everything. I know when I was working; my greatest successes were the result of giving it my all. I sought the assistance of others when I needed it and did my best to help them be their best.

In 2021, I'll try to be kinder, listen to more music, dance more often, sing louder (and on key), read more widely, be a better friend, touch more softly, play harder, walk more briskly, care with passion, be thankful for every day, and do all of the above "like I mean it."

## Chapter 37

## Wise Beyond Her Years

My granddaughter, Eva, is ten and a half going on thirty-two. She's bright and full of life. She knows what she likes and what she doesn't like. She isn't afraid to share her thoughts. You may not always agree with what she has to say, but you can be sure that anything that she has to share is worth "the listen."

She's a talented girl with many interests: singing, dancing, softball, gymnastics, basketball, drawing, swimming, water skiing, magic, teaching school, and baking with her dad.

I spent the night with Eva, Brady and their mom, Lindsay, a week or so ago. (Dad was out-of-town.) When I got out of my morning shower, Eva made me a cup of coffee and a piece of toast and jelly. (Add short order cook to resumé.) We had a conversation about the possibility that Ruth and I might sell our home at the lake and look for a smaller house or condo in Michigan. While we were talking, Eva looked up a house on Zillow for us to buy. One of her selling points was, "It's in my friend, Emily's, subdivision and I could ride my bike over to visit you." Now we can add "real estate consultant" to the list of her many talents.

A few days ago, Eva invited me to join with others in editing a story that she is writing for school. It's called "Playing in the Mud." While the story does need editing, the lesson she offers is way beyond her years. She began her tale by asking...

*Have you ever felt nervous and excited at the same time or felt like suddenly fireworks are going off? That has happened to me when playing in the mud and the thoughts of getting in trouble crossed my mind a thousand times. You finally realize it's okay to get messy in your life because it wouldn't be fun if no one did things that weren't easy for them. So we can tell the stories, live the adventure, and learn the lessons of a lifetime. Sometimes all it takes is to step a little outside of your comfort zone.*

I've had the feeling that she questions. I've been nervous and excited. I have felt like "fireworks were going off." I expect that you have too. It's a part of life. As Eva points out, it's "okay to get messy" because that's part of the *fun* of living life. Try new things. Explore. Do things that may not be easy. Life is a series of stories strung together that include a multitude of lessons. "Stepping outside of your comfort zone" adds excitement to the journey. The challenge for each of us is to live a good story.

While I have only chosen a portion of her story to share, Eva's tale about playing in the mud includes her friend Natalee. She provides details to her adventure with her friend and the risks that they embark on with each other. The excitement of trying something new outweighed the possibility that they might get in trouble.

*If I hadn't gone down to the creek, and hadn't had Natalee over, I wouldn't have learned that it is okay to get messy. I now know and it's a great memory to hold on to for a lifetime. I'm so happy I did it. I hope you liked my story and learned along with me. Meanwhile, I still have a lot to learn. Lastly, I hope you remember it's okay to get messy. Just remember, always have fun.*

Risk taking is a part of life. My advice moving forward is to weigh the risk against the reward. Sitting still, and attempting nothing new, is indeed safer than taking the risk but as Eva points out, "getting messy" creates "great memories." We all "still have a lot to learn" and we should "always have fun."

Great advice from a young lady who's wise beyond her years.

## Chapter 38

## My Resourceful Father

My grandson, Brady, has started doing work for pay. I saw him at Christmas, and he told me that he and a friend had started a business raking leaves and shoveling snow for their neighbors. They worked in tandem and picked up their jobs by offering their services to carefully selected prospective clients. They were making money.

When I was in Michigan last month, I asked how things had progressed. He itemized his jobs for me and outlined how much he made on each one. The income started at $20.00 and rose to as high as $50.00. Not bad for a couple of twelve-year olds.

He and his family spent the Easter holiday with us in Florida. I asked again how business was going and how he sets his price for a job. He told me that he just allows the market to determine his pay. Customers pay him what they believe his services are worth. I hope to hire him for assistance with my yard spring clean-up duties when I return to Michigan.

As Brady shared his job responsibilities, it reminded me of my early working career and some of the jobs I had. Although I didn't bore him with all the tasks I have performed over the years, I did tell him of a time that I worked with my dad on a lawn project.

All the houses on our street were designed the same. The lots were 50 by 125 with a sidewalk that divided the front 50 in half and led up to a front porch with two steps. A few of the fancier houses had a covered entrance that projected over the same type of front porch. My friend, Bill Graham, lived in one of those. There were only three or four more houses with the fancy porch on the entire block.

One year after my dad hit it big in a poker game, (that's probably not true but does offer up an explanation how he got the cash for a home improvement project) my parents had the front walk and original porch torn off. It was a perfectly good front porch, but they wanted something different. They replaced the porch with a larger, longer porch that stretched across about two-thirds of the house and ended with two, top of the line, pre-cast steps leading down to the driveway. It was big for the neighborhood. But that wasn't enough. They added a black, wrought-iron railing and topped it off with a huge green and white awning that covered the entire porch. The green awning was a beautiful accent that complemented the white-sided house. I believe everyone on our block has suffered "porch envy" ever since.

Once the remodeled porch was complete, my dad tackled the torn up front yard. The sidewalk was gone, the remaining yard was a mess, so something had to be done. Dad decided to have new topsoil delivered and the newly manicured front yard would be topped off with beautiful Kentucky Blue grass sod. (Cha Ch'ing!!!) Before the sod could be installed, the manicuring had to take place. The new topsoil guys delivered the topsoil. The responsibility for spreading the topsoil (by shovel) and the leveling (by rake) fell upon my dad and his "right-hand man" (me). Dad spent a couple of evenings after work shoveling dirt. The balance of the shoveling, and all the raking, was handled on Saturday (my one free day without school or church).

While **all** of my friends were preparing for a Saturday full of baseball down at the park, I got to do yard work. I was a reluctant eleven-year-old "right-hand man." In addition to my involuntary recruitment, I found out that seven and four-year old girls do not have to do yard work.

Now that the sidewalk was gone, the yard was huge! It was 50 feet wide and about 20 feet deep! There was also a side yard that was another 10 feet wide and 20 feet deep. Can you say **GIGANTIC**! **ALL** of it had to be raked. If reincarnation is a real thing, my dad was probably a plantation owner in a prior life.

I started raking on the driveway side of the yard while my dad spread the remaining topside on the side yard. Shoveling looked more fun than raking. The goal of raking was to provide a nice level surface for the new sod. The sod was going to be delivered Monday afternoon, so we only had two days to complete the raking. My first thought was that we would probably have to rake day and night to get it done. Not only did we have to rake the soil, but it had to be clump free. If I found a clump of dirt, I had to break it down by hand. If I found a rock, or even the tiny, tiniest, little pebble, I had to place it in a pail. Dad wanted a clump-free and bump-free level surface for his new sod.

After dad finished the shoveling, he started to help with the raking. This was about the same time that the guys were walking by the house to see if I could play ball. I couldn't. As the guys passed, my dad yelled, "Hey, Rob. Look what I found!" He held up a nickel.

"Where did you find it?" I asked.

"Right here where I was raking."

He started raking again and as soon as he started, he said, "Holy Cow! I found a dime!"

I started raking harder and faster. If he was finding money, there must be some on my side of the yard. My dad's new-found wealth stopped the ball players in their tracks.

One of the boys asked, "Mr. Tebo, can I rake too?"

"Sure, if you have a rake." (My dad liked to include everyone in his chores. He had a big heart and liked to help the kids whenever he could.)

In about five minutes, Bill Graham, Mark Conti, Bobby and Bruce Matson, and three of the Prested boys were raking side by side. Baseball gloves, balls and bats were lying on the driveway and topsoil was flying. An armored car must have crashed into the topsoil yard because the guys were finding pennies, nickels, dimes and a couple of lucky quarters as the topsoil got smoother and smoother. There were so many boys raking that there wasn't room in the yard for my dad, so he had to stop. He did walk around to make sure that everyone was doing a good job. That was the day that I discovered what being a supervisor was all about.

It turns out seven boys can rake a yard faster than a dad and his "right-hand man." We finished the raking before noon. When we boys counted up our discovery, we must have had a total of three or four dollars.

As we were picking up our balls, bats, and gloves, and getting ready to head to the park, our neighbor, Mrs. Barkery, brought out some cookies and lemonade to her husband who was working in his yard. We dropped the baseball gear, picked up our rakes, and joined Mr. Barkery. Turns out we liked cookies and lemonade almost as much as the almighty dollar.

## Chapter 39

## Learn Something New

Last year, Ruth and I bought a new dining room set for our home in Florida. I even wrote a blog about the purchase. Our tables have been the centerpiece of wonderful conversations over our years together. When we returned this year, Ruth noticed "the leg on your chair is wobbly." She called the furniture store and they said they'd send a repairman. "He'll be in touch with you." Later that day he called and set an appointment for December 31st.

When the man and woman team arrived, I pointed out a small dent on the underside of one corner of the table that we discovered after it was delivered last year. We didn't do anything about it at the time, but since they were on site, I asked if this was something they could address. The helper spoke right up, "I can take care of that." Carlos and his helper completed their tasks in about fifteen minutes. Everything is as good as new.

We talked a bit before they left about their jobs as subcontractors for the furniture store. Carlos said, "We don't make furniture in the United States anymore, so no one here knows how to fix it. I learned from my brother, and she (as he referred to his helper) learned from her father. There are no schools teaching this." We discussed the importance of learning by doing. "If it weren't for my brother, and her dad, we wouldn't have these jobs today. People would be discarding more things instead of fixing them. We do too much of that."

When they left, I thought about some of the things I learned from the adults in my life. I learned how to cook by watching my dad. He wasn't a great cook by anyone's measure, but he did cook. It was a natural part of our home. While we had cereal most mornings during the week, Dad would fry bacon and eggs on the weekend, or hamburgers on Saturday nights. His mix featured bits of chopped onion. It wasn't what he made that impressed me, but that he did indeed cook. He also scrubbed the kitchen floor, ran the vacuum, ironed his own work shirts, and sewed on a missing button or two. The lesson was men work around the house as well as women.

He wasn't particularly handy, but he tackled many jobs just the same. If it required muscle like building a driveway, tearing out and planting shrubs, or putting in a new lawn, he was right at home. He knew, too, when things were best left to others, so he deferred to my Grandpa Barner if the furnace was on the fritz (a technical term for broken). When the house needed to be remodeled, or a new roof, he called upon my Uncle Harry Barner. I got to watch them all, so I learned from the best. Like my dad, I learned when I was comfortable tackling something new. I also learned the hard way, through failure, when it was best to rely upon others.

The summer I turned sixteen, I worked with Grandpa Barner in his plumbing and heating business. I learned about the various types of wrenches: pipe, combination, socket, basin, monkey, and open-end. More importantly, I learned how to use them. I also learned how to clean furnaces and hang duct work. I mastered tin snips and hack saws. The most important lesson of the summer was I'd rather make a living with my brain than my muscles. I wouldn't have learned that if I hadn't had the chance to work with Grandpa.

Ruth and my first home was a two-unit house that I bought the second year I taught. When I bought it, I painted the upstairs unit. I learned how to paint by doing. After we married, we moved into the lower unit. It was short on closets, so Ruth's dad, Lou, built two matching closets on either side of the large window that faced the street side of the house. He was a professional carpenter. I "held," "fetched," but mostly "watched" how he attacked his task. I learned as I watched, so when other similar jobs arose over the years, I was able to "do."

At one point I noticed the floor near our toilet was beginning to sag. I knew how to pull the toilet from my work with my grandfather. When I told Lou what I was planning to do, he offered to help. "If the floor is sagging, you'll have to cut out the bad spot and replace the underlayment." That's the day I learned about "underlayment." We pulled the toilet and identified the area that needed to be replaced. Lou used a drill to cut a pilot hole and placed his jigsaw in the hole. He cut out the bad spot, then measured and cut a piece of plywood to replace it. When it didn't quite fit, he took a piece of scrap wood to use as a buffer and tapped on it with a hammer until the new piece fell into place. I would have beat on the new piece until it fit, but Lou knew better. I've used that trick dozens of times over the past fifty years.

The women in my life started with my mom. I guess that's true for most, but I know not all. If we've known our mothers, we're very lucky.

Many of my mother's lessons were unintentional. For example, she taught me dancing was fun. I could see how much she enjoyed it when she danced with her sister, Ruth. They danced wonderfully together. The faster, the better. My dad danced too, but I don't recall him dancing fast. He was more of a "hold 'em close" kinda guy.

When she was cooking, we three kids could help if we liked. She showed me how to measure and mix, dice and chop, and the difference between stirring and whisking. Whisking makes egg whites fluffy. That's a lesson everyone should learn.

She let me cook with the aid of her *Betty Crocker Cookbook*. I excelled at making meatballs. One Sunday, when I was about twelve, as I was making meatballs and spaghetti for our family, my Aunt Bern and her crew arrived. We had more burger, so I made more meatballs. While making the second batch, Aunt Gert and the twins showed, so I made even more. We had a meal for about a dozen.

The spaghetti sauce called for stewed tomatoes. Mom knew I didn't like their texture (kinda reminded me of boogers), so she told me I could run them through our food mill. The hand crank contraption turned the tomatoes into puree. I could eat them that way. The big takeaway was "there's always room for more at our kitchen table."

My Grandma Tebo moved in with us after Grandpa Tebo died. I was eight. The three kids shared the upstairs while Mom and Dad and Grandma had the two bedrooms on the main level. She wore "house dresses" and aprons. She had two pairs of shoes. Both were black leather high tops with a dozen eyelets on either side. The only difference between the two pairs was their age. She helped my mom around the house with the cooking and sewing. She darned my dad's white work socks by slipping a shot glass in the sock to provide a backing for her needlework. She created beautiful quilts of her own design. Every stitch was done by hand. More than one had a back made from flour sacks. The fronts were created from colorful leftover pieces of cloth or repurposed dresses. The corner of each piece was hand-tied.

Grandma did a lot of cooking. She made everything from scratch. If you gave her a "box mix" she probably wouldn't know what to do with it. Baking was her specialty. She did it all...cakes, pies, coffee cake, cookies, bread, noodles for her chicken soup, and the best cinnamon rolls on earth. She used our Formica topped kitchen table to roll everything out. She floured the tabletop so nothing would stick, and she let the flour fly.

She let my sister, Sharron, and me help. When Jackie got older, she pitched in too, but the beginning was mostly Sharron and me. Grandma would give us our own dough to work with. We filled our miniature pies with jelly she and my mom made. The raspberries and grapes came from our backyard, and dad brought the strawberries home from Eastern Market. We sprinkled cinnamon and sugar on our cookies and decorated whatever we wanted with raisins and red cinnamon candies. While I knew I could never hope to achieve her level of success, I enjoyed the opportunity to bake my own creations.

Grandma Barner died when I was eleven. She was my "rich" grandma. She was always "dressed up." She wore nylons, earrings, and heels. She had a mink stole and the minks still had their eyes. I was fascinated by the fact that she polished her nails. They were bright red like most of her lipsticks. She and Grandma Tebo were both born in 1899, but by the time I got to know them, they were two different women living two different lifestyles.

Grandma Barner was an artist. Her first creations were paint-by-number oil paintings she purchased from the local art store. When I took an interest in her handiwork, she bought me my own set. While she went on to paint beautiful pieces of china, I was one and done with my paint by number kit. Ruth and I, and Elizabeth and Sutton, have a couple of her oil paintings hanging in our homes.

During her "china years," she produced dozens of beautiful hand painted plates, cups and saucers. gravy boats with ladles, and fancy china clocks. As I got older, I realized how talented she was. Luckily, I have several pieces to pass on to David, Elizabeth, and Michael.

She crocheted doilies and sewed elaborate embroidered works. When I took an interest in her embroidery, she found white muslin fabric, cut it into pieces the size of dish cloths, and then drew pictures of animals and flowers on the cloth. She locked her drawings in embroidery hoops, let me choose the color thread I wished to work with, and turned me loose. I only sewed for one afternoon, but I've used what I learned that day ever since.

Grandma raised violets and guppies on her back sunroom. She had several aquariums and dozens of pots with delicate purple flowers. Through her lessons I learned fish had babies, and you must move them to tanks away from their parents because the adults will eat their young. She grew new plants in small glasses of water. Once the roots developed, she planted the newbies in pots, and repeated the process over and over. She taught me, if you care for things, they will thrive.

I was raised in a simpler time. Things didn't move as fast as they do today. I think the old way may have been better.

My first teachers were my parents, grandparents, aunts and uncles, and my parents' friends. They provided lessons no matter what their intention. As children, we tend to follow the lead of significant adults, those we interact with on a regular basis. For me, many of those lessons took place at our dinner table and family gatherings. Most involved a meal, or ice cream and cake, at somebody's something. People actually spoke to one another.

When I was a child, my dad often worked past dinner time, so we ate without him. Mom always had a plate for him when he got home, and she sat with him as he ate while sharing the news of the day. When he did get home in time for dinner, and always on the weekend, we ate as a family. During our meals I did a lot of listening. My parents spoke of current events, made plans for the weekend, and discussed which relative was about to celebrate what.

I learned a lot from the adults in my life. They taught me how to cook, sew, care for people more than things, save, build, be open to new ideas, repair, mentor, the difference between right and wrong, how to keep time with the music, grow, play, show affection, not to gamble with more than you can afford to lose, read, cipher and write, explore, which tools to use for what project, have patience, listen more than you speak, and the list goes on.

The most important lesson was "never stop learning." Listen to others, consider new ideas, and ultimately, decide which path to follow. Make a difference. Take risks. Making mistakes is a part of growing. The trick is trying to avoid making the same mistakes over and over.

Ruth and I have tried to pass these skills and values to David, Elizabeth, and Michael. So far, so good. They are good people, making a difference in the lives of those around them. They've taken different paths, and we celebrate that too. We've had the opportunity to share our time, and outlook, with Brady and Eva, and are looking forward to doing the same with young Jackson when he arrives.

No matter who we are, or what we accomplish, each of us should strive to leave this world a little better than we found it.

## Chapter 40

## My Three Wise Men

In 1995 I gave a journal to each of my parents as a Christmas gift and asked them to record stories from their past. I have my father's journal. My request of him reads as follows:

*Dad – you, Uncle Harry Mac and Uncle Harry Barner have shared dozens of tales from your youth. I love hearing them. Please use this book to write them down so our family will always to able to know "how it used to be." I'll get you more books if you need them! Love Rob*

He wrote on thirteen pages of the journal. The first four-page entry was written on that first Christmas Day. The last nine pages were written over the last nine months of his life while he was in an assortment hospitals and nursing facilities. His handwriting became less legible as his health failed. Most of the final nine pages were about current events – things that he was witnessing during those nine months.

My dad and Uncle Harry Mac were best friends for most of their lives. My dad described Uncle Harry as more of a brother than a friend. I'm not sure how, or where, they met. I know they loved and respected one another until their final days.

The beginning of my dad's journal reads as follows:

*Christmas 1995 Please excuse some of the spelling as you all know your dad didn't do very good in school.*

*I met your uncle Harry Mac I believe it was around 1938. We never had much money but whatever we had we would share right down the center.*

*We dated a lot together with your mom and Aunt Ruth. At that time Uncle Harry had very little eyesight so when he would get a letter from Aunt Ruth, I would read it for him and add a few extra lines. He would say, "That's not really in there." And I would say "It sure is."*

*We would always borrow, or should I say rent, a car from one of our friends. But we never paid the rent.*

Throughout my childhood, my college years, and beyond I had the opportunity to share time with the three most important men in my life: my dad and my two Uncle Harrys. Uncle Harry Barner was the younger brother of my mom (Kay) and Aunt Ruth. When they spoke, I listened. I didn't always follow their advice, but I knew they always had my best interest at heart. I think I learned more from the story of their lives than the advice that they offered. I listened to their words but watched their deeds.

All three men told a similar story that took place when Harry Barner was twelve or thirteen. My dad and Uncle Harry Mac had gone out on a date with young Harry's older sisters, Kate and Ruth. They had spent the evening dancing and drinking beer. I expect that the girls did most of the dancing and the guys consumed most of the beer. In any case, after everyone returned to the girl's home a dangerous storm hit the area. My grandfather consented to allowing the two suitors to spend the night so that they would remain safe. There was one condition. They had to share a bed with young Harry and Harry was charged to insure that his two elders remained with him throughout the night.

They went to bed with Harry Barner sandwiched between his two sisters' boyfriends. My dad and Uncle Harry Mac were down for the count. Beer will do that to a fella. It will also create a great gaseous disruption. Harry Barner's version of the story ended with my dad farting on his left, Harry Mac farting on his right, and him wishing he had a larger bed.

My three wise men operated through a common theme. Family first. They worked to ensure that each of their children was ready to face the world, but they expected each child to be able make it on his/her own.

The last time that I was with Uncle Harry Mac and my dad, I took my dad to visit Uncle Harry in the hospital. Neither was doing very well. My dad was in a nursing home and Uncle Harry in the hospital. The day of our visit Uncle Harry was in rehab. His daughter, my cousin Ruth Ann, was with him. As Uncle Harry went through his exercise program, my dad joined him. They did the same exercises. One was required to participate and the other joined his friend. There were a series of pulls and stretches and a mini obstacle course. I felt like I was witnessing a mini Olympics. The final event was a set of three stairs that led to a platform and back down three more on the other side. After completing the stairway walk they both sat down, side by side, held hands and never said a word.

Within a few weeks both of their conditions deteriorated. They died ten days apart. Uncle Harry on June 17 and dad on June 27th. Those two dates were sandwiched around Father's Day June 20th, 1999.

Last June Uncle Harry Barner passed. He turned 89 on June 13th and passed on the 26th. His birthday and passing fell on both sides of Father's Day June 18th, 2017. He was laid to rest on June 30, exactly eighteen years to the day that we buried my dad.

I had the honor of serving as a pallbearer for each of these men. It was tough duty but an important part of my life. I helped carry each of these uncommon men to a common field.

I'm thankful for the lessons they taught me and the stories that they've shared. I think on this Father's Day they would want me to share their most important life lesson which was that *each of us should do our best to live a good story.*

## Chapter 41

## Ed at 100

I met Ed a little over ten years ago. Our first meeting was not a happy one. We met in a funeral home where I came to pay my respects to a friend of mine whose mother had died. Ed is his dad.

Ed was ninety years old when we met. He turns 100 today, November 19, 2017. Ed is the only person that I have ever known to reach that mark. Ed still lives alone, drives a car, plays golf, and plays poker with a group of us every other week.

His poker buddies are 30 years younger and Ed loves playing with the "kids." He sometimes stays in hands longer than he should and has been heard to say, "I've got just enough to suck me in." More importantly, we love playing poker with him. He reminds us through his presence that we too have a lot of good years ahead of us.

Old age looks more promising when you have someone like Ed to emulate. We never discuss this, but I expect that he has become a second father to most of us whose fathers have passed.

He doesn't hit a golf ball as far as he once did, but he has great putting skills. He plays at a local course several times a week. Most of his peers have passed so he ends up playing with a group of 80-year-olds. More kids in his life to hang with.

Last year the poker group was playing one of its annual golf matches and one of the guys couldn't make it. I asked a friend of mine, Russ, to join us. Russ and Ed played in the same foursome and seventy-three-year-old Russ told Ed that he had presented his high school diploma to him at his graduation some fifty-five years earlier. Ed was the president of the local schoolboard and presented all such honors as the students graduated. Small world and a long time.

I think the most interesting thing about Ed is that he still works. While it's true that he retired in 1984, he bought a couple of machine tools six years prior and put them in his garage. When he "retired," he started doing contract work for a couple of manufacturers who keep Ed in the game by sending small parts to be processed on a regular basis. He has done this "side job" for over thirty years and continues to do so today. It's hard to keep a good man down.

Ed has become my hero. As I grow up, I want to be like him. Self-sufficient and engaged in activities that I love. While he has slowed down a bit, his life is still active and filled with people he loves and who love him.

Happy birthday, Ed.

## Chapter 42

## Ed at 103

This is the fourth time I've written about Ed's birthday. I hope to write at least a dozen more. He turned 103 last Thursday. After our successful move north, I drove back to play poker with the boys to celebrate the event.

The poker game was much like our other games except this time we sang to our senior member. Like always, the group shared a lot of stories. Ed mentioned that he had read my most recent blog about getting turned down for a date. He shared that he had similar fears in his youth. He liked to dance but was afraid of getting turned down when asking a girl. As he spoke, I flashed back to the dances I attended at Clara Barton Junior High. The boys gathered on one side of the gym and the girls on the other. I imagined Ed standing next to me, taking a deep breath, and making that long walk across the gym floor hoping the girl with the pretty blue eyes would say "yes."

Ed has seen more of life than any of us. Woodrow Wilson was president when he was born. We've had a total of 18 presidents during his lifetime. That's almost a third of our country's history. The Spanish Flu, with its estimated 20 – 50 million world-wide deaths, ran its course during his second year. The coronavirus during his 103rd year, and its current world-wide death total standing just north of 1.4 million, is a distant second. He's seen both.

Each summer the poker group plays golf together at least once. This year with the coronavirus lurking about, we played just nine holes. We teed it up at Ed's home course, Sharp Park, in Jackson. We had two teams of four, and I was fortunate to be on Ed's winning team. We played a modified scramble. Each player hit a drive, the team chose the best shot, and each of us played our own ball in from that spot. Everyone got one mulligan to use anywhere on the course. Ed's not one to brag, but I will. On the second hole, a par three, Ed attempted a 20-foot putt from the fringe. He missed. He used his mulligan and sank his second attempt. Birdie for us.

A few holes later, he sank another 20-plus footer to save par, but my favorite shot of the day was Ed's last. I was standing with him about twenty yards short of the green. He turned to me and said, "Back in the day, I would chip this up and get close enough to tap it in. Up and down in two." And then I said, "You're older and wiser now. Just chip it in!" So, he did! Amazing!

There's an old phrase I first heard in my youth… Steady Eddie. If you check out the urban dictionary, you'll read things like "reliable," "straight forward," and "a man you can always count on." What you see is what you get. That's Ed. He's not flashy or pretentious. He's just a man who keeps on keeping on, and I'm very proud that he is my friend.

## Chapter 43

## Ed at 105

My first blog was called "Ed." I published it on November 19, 2017. It was my first attempt at writing for an audience. It was about my friend who turned 100 years old that day. He turned again yesterday. He's 105. No matter how long I live, I'll never meet another man like him. He just keeps on keeping on. He lives a simple life, and it's served him well.

He hasn't played golf since he broke his hip a couple years ago, and he uses a walker to get around. But younger men, and women, have done the same.

I called Ed yesterday and we visited a bit. Every time we speak, whether it's at a poker game, or on the phone, he tells me he reads and enjoys my blog. I enjoy writing for him. Most of my recent stories have had a somber tone. I've been writing about losing Ruth while doing my best to honor her memory. Writing about Ed is a celebration.

During our phone conversation, he recounted his last poker game with the guys. He admitted he had a run of bad luck and went through all his cash early in the evening. He dug into his "emergency stash." He cashed in a $100 bill one of his bosses gave him back in the day for emergencies. Ed retired in the late seventies, so I'm not sure his boss thought being down in a poker game was an "emergency," but Ed did.

His son, Craig, cashed the bill for him. Craig knew it was special. By the end of the evening, Ed was able to buy the bill back. He's probably stuffed it back in his wallet for another decade.

He and his family went out to dinner last night. If the Common Grill provides a birthday discount for its customers, they're going to owe Ed some money. Five percent of his bill to be exact.

I asked Ed if there were any secrets to his longevity. His reply was, "Not really. I try to keep my nose clean and take one day at a time." That's good advice for all of us.

When we met, Ed was ninety years old, and to tell you the truth, other than the walker, he doesn't look much older than the night we met. I guess good looks level off after a while.

Happy birthday, Ed.

# Chapter 44

# If I Were You I'd

As I entered my adult years, my dad had a habit of offering up the phrase, "If I were you I'd..." The words that completed the phrase were his unsolicited advice. He'd tell my sisters, or me, what we should do given a certain situation.

"If I were you I'd save the money until you can pay cash for the vacation that you're planning."

"If I were you I'd wait until the (insert item) goes on sale."

"If I were you I'd think twice before doing that."

He offered up his advice to help us. He wasn't trying to control our lives, but he wanted to make sure that we considered all of our options (or at least the options that he'd consider) before taking action. He was looking out for our well-being without telling us what to do. "If I was you, I'd..." was a softer approach.

Over the years I sometimes followed, but mostly dismissed, his advice. The one big takeaway for me was when he said, "I don't care what you decide to do, but whatever it is, do your best. If you want to dig ditches, dig the best ones." He truly meant that.

Most of the time I chose to watch his actions rather than heed his words. What he *did* was more important to me than what he told me to do. By observing I learned many things but among the most important were to...

1. Provide for my wife and children.
2. Work hard.
3. Share.
4. Take turns.
5. Have fun.
6. Be kind to *all* children.

I know that I took away more than those six items, but those come to mind as I write this today.

My version of "If I was you I'd..." sounds like "I don't know anything about...but have you ever considered...?" I'm very sure that I offered up the occasional "What the he— are you thinking?", but I try not to. I do think that I've done a better job of avoiding "What the...?", since the kids have started families of their own.

Advice is a tricky thing. While I expect that most of it is well intended, it's not always well received. Telling is a lot easier than doing. I think that the best advice I ever received was simply, "Do the right thing." The challenge is to determine what the "right thing" is before you take action. Being kind is probably always the "right thing to do."

A couple of months ago, shortly before Ruth and I headed south, and shortly after my friend Jim passed, my granddaughter, Eva, and Ruth were discussing a challenge that Eva had experienced. The discussion turned to "being kind" and doing the "right thing." Out of the blue Eva offered up this observation, "Jim would never *be* unkind." Jim never spoke to her about kindness, but Eva always watched.

As I enter a new year I do so knowing that I have received good advice from two important men and *doing* the right thing is always the best thing. I also know that their lessons are as important to my granddaughter's generation as they are to mine.

## Chapter 45

## For One Hour

There are several popular posts appearing on Facebook. There's one about golf that keeps popping up. It asks you to name your dream foursome. For me that's always been easy, I'd choose my three kids, David, Elizabeth, Michael and me. Ruth's recent resurgence on the links muddies the waters a bit, but if we couldn't go out as a five some, I'd still go with the kids. Getting the three of them together to do anything is a challenge, so I'd grab the opportunity. If the rules guy said that I had to choose professional golfers, I'd pick Freddie Couples, Phil Mickelson, and Arnie.

I saw another question the other day that asked, "If you could talk to someone for one hour, who would you choose?" There's a number of good options: great orators, religious figures, Nobel prize winners, human rights leaders, political figures, sports personalities, scientists, explorers, inventors. The list of options is endless. When I asked Ruth who she'd opt for, she said, "Jesus." That's a great choice.

I didn't have to ponder the options very long. If I had such an hour, I'd choose my dad. He'll be gone for twenty-one years later this month. His final months were confined to hospitals and nursing homes, and while those months were terrible for him, they were good for me. I visited with him almost every week. We spoke one on one, took drives to visit family members, went out to eat, played cards, and on most occasions, we shared stories. I let him do most of the talking, and I just listened. I let him direct the path our conversations took as I didn't wish to bring up memories that might be upsetting. During our talks, I validated my beliefs about him and heard a few new tales.

If I could choose the place, I'd opt for St. Peters Church Cemetery in Mt. Clemens, Michigan. It's a quiet place so I expect we'd be able to speak privately. We visited the cemetery on one of our drives because that's where his birth mother, Nettie, and his grandparents, Mary and George are buried. Dad was fourteen years old when he helped dig his mother's grave.

During our visit I learned that my extended family is larger than I thought. George Tebo had one brother that I knew, Art. During our visit to the cemetery, Dad spoke of eight children: Vern, John, George, Alfred, Dudley, Art, Maud, and Jess. I asked him to write their names on a slip of paper so I wouldn't forget. With six male Tebos, it's no wonder I've been asked several times if I'm related to so and so. I probably am.

During our hour I'd try to learn more about my extended family. My guess is he's told me what he knows; otherwise, we would have discussed it during our fifty-two years together. But if he had more to share, I'd love to hear it.

The first question I'd ask is pretty straight forward. In a complicated world, it's pretty simple. Dad didn't make it to many of my ball games. He worked long hours and seldom got home in time. I played football in eighth and tenth grades. He never made it to any of those. I played organized baseball for a half dozen years, and he may have made it to about that many games. I remember one game in particular, because one of the umpires didn't show up. The coaches recruited Dad to ump first base. He hadn't been to any of my games that year, so I didn't think he'd recognize me in my uniform.

On my first trip to the plate I pulled the ball to third. I've never been fleet of foot, but I managed to make it fast enough to make it a bang – bang play. Dad called me safe, and the opposing coach, Mr. Sura, moaned, "Ah, come on Tony." I think I was safe. I'm sure my foot hit the bag before I heard the ball hit the glove, but I'd asked Dad if I really made it or he just ruled in my favor.

I'd tell him about David, Elizabeth and Michael and the great partners they've chosen. I'd show him a picture of Brady and Eva and brag a bit about them. I'd also show him two other pictures, one of him as a young man and another of our Michael (Dad called him Frenchy). I think they look alike, and they both resemble Tony Jerome.

But most of the hour, I'd like to hear anything he wished to share. I think I'm a better listener now than I was twenty-one years ago. I'm not focused on my job, striking deals, earning money, or concerned about the kids making it through college. I listened pretty well at work but wasn't always tuned in with my family.

I'd like to know his views on what's happening today. Most of all, I'd like to hear his voice. I remember how it changed over the years. His tone grew weaker as he aged. I sometimes hear my voice do the same.

He wasn't a yeller. He spoke and expected you to follow along. He offered up a lot of "If I were you" words of advice. I'd like to hear it all again, because now that I'm older, I might agree more often.

Vulgar language was not his style, but he wasn't perfect in that respect. He offered up a few GDs but most were through frustration rather than anger. I dropped an F-bomb once during a poker game at my cousins, Bob and Beverly's, house. It's the only time I swore in his presence. I was well into my twenties, and had too much to drink, but he still let me know my words were unacceptable. He was right.

I've got pieces of his stories stored in my brain. I'd like to have him retell them so I could lock the entire truth together. We loved many of the same people and I'd like to speak of them again. The more I write, the more I remember. It's both a blessing and a curse. It makes me happy to recall those who loved me but makes me miss them more.

You've made it this far through my tale, so let me offer an "If I was you..." that I think Dad and I would share. "If I was you, and you still have an hour to speak with someone, take advantage of it, even if you do it in a dozen five-minute chunks."

I'm certain you won't regret it, but you may if you don't.

# Section Three

## My Sudden Surprise

## Chapter 46

## The Back of the Cards

I enjoy playing cards. I got the bug from my parents. Mom played pinochle with a group of friends for several years. They rotated the host site from lady to lady. They played for a few hours and ate fancy snacks and desserts. When they played at our house, my sisters and I got the leftovers.

Dad played poker. The only time I saw him in action was when he played with my uncles and their friends, but I know he traveled to his work friends' homes for more action. That's how I got the poker bug. When I was old enough to handle the pressure, they dealt me in.

Mom gave me my first card lesson when I was about eleven. My parents rented a cottage on Commerce Lake for a couple of summers. Dad drove to work from the cottage, and my sisters and I stayed with Mom to play in the lake. The cottage was a large room with a very small bathroom. There were a couple of wires running across the room with sheets on hooks. The sheets designated the bedrooms and were the only privacy in the cottage.

Dad didn't get home some nights until well after the girls were in bed, and with no TV, Mom and I played 500 rummy and pinochle on the cottage porch. We didn't disturb the girls that way. She taught me the rules, and I was hooked. I've played cards ever since.

I have the same guidelines my dad did. I just want to know the rules before we shuffle up and deal. I've played all sorts of games. Some involve wagers, some just bragging rights.

Playing games involves a bit of strategy. In addition to knowing the rules, you have to determine the best way to play the cards you're dealt. If you play with the same people, you learn a bit about their tendencies. That comes in handy in determining your next play. Good players have options. They have a plan B should plan A fail.

I've often thought the greatest challenge in any card game is the back of the cards. You know what you have, but you're never really sure about your opponents. You can hazard a guess, and even try to count the cards, but being wrong leads to failure.

Many of the lessons learned at the card table can be transferred to life. You can lay out a plan based upon what you know to be true (the front of the cards). But life doesn't always go the way you plan when what you thought might be true, turns out to be incorrect. (The back of the cards.)

Some people avoid certain games because they don't win often enough. If they took the same stance with everything in their life, they'd never have any fun. You can't always know what's going to happen next, but you can carry forward with the things you know to be true. We've got to be ready to change our course when things don't go as planned. That's what makes life interesting.

## Chapter 47

## Sorry For Your Loss

There's no easy way to start this next series of blogs. I've struggled with the words, but none seem to work. Ruth was involved in a car accident last Tuesday evening, and she died. This is the first time I've used the word. It's too final.

If you've read her obituary, you may think I wrote it. I didn't. Michael's wife, Kate, did. I tweaked a personal message she sent me. The only thing I added was a few words about Kate. David, Elizabeth, Michael, and I discussed Ruth's obituary, and as Elizabeth said, "It needs to be spicy." When I read Kate's text, we had the words.

The kids and I have received a number of calls and texts offering words of support. They're welcome and helpful. It's good to know others loved Ruth like us. How could you not?

Some have said, "We're sorry for your loss." While I believe their words are sincere, people also want to know what happened. We're a curious breed.

Ruth was driving home from Mt. Pleasant when she had a "medical emergency." That's what the two State Police officers said when they rang the doorbell. I already knew something was wrong as she was late, and she was never late. I was told she'd lost consciousness, veered off the road, and hit a parked car. Medical personnel tried to revive her, but their efforts failed, and she was pronounced dead at the scene. By the time they found me, Ruth had been taken to the medical examiner's office at Sparrow Hospital in Lansing.

That's all I knew when I called the kids. David, then Michael, and finally, Elizabeth. I did my best to hold it together through each call. I lost it while speaking with Elizabeth. "Now that I've told you, Elizabeth, I can cry."

I used the word "gone" in each conversation. "Your mom's gone." "Gone" was easier than dead. "Gone" gave me hope.

When I started this blog five years ago, I wanted my grandchildren to have a written record of their extended family. I had listened to stories in my youth, remembered many, and wanted them to live on. Not all stories have happy endings. While Ruth's life is over, her legacy will live on through her children and grandchildren, and I'll do my best to honor her memory.

There've been many times when I've written and asked her to review before I hit "publish." Several times she said, "You can't write that. It's too controversial." or "That word's too raw, you've got to change it." Most of the time, I'd rethink my idea and follow her suggestion. Now that I don't have her to be my censor, I apologize in advance if I offend you. That's not my intent. I have strong feelings about a lot of things, and I don't always censor myself as she thought I should.

I've had dozens of conversations on the phone the past week. There have been two occasions when I was about to say something unkind about someone and the call dropped. I could still hear the caller, but they couldn't hear me. There's no doubt in my mind that Ruth was intervening.

My next several posts will be about Ruth. Writing is my therapy. If you don't already, I hope you learn to love her as I do. You can't get enough of a good thing.

## Chapter 48

## Something More

The day Ruth died was like any other day we shared. She was up earlier than me, so she ate early, and I ate late. We spoke like we did thousands of other retired mornings. If I wasn't out golfing early, we talked, played a game of Euchre, and reviewed our individual days. Golf was canceled this day, we didn't take time for Euchre, and we spoke just long enough to share our plans for the day.

For the past few months, a group of guys played poker at our place every other Tuesday evening. She'd go to the casino in Mt. Pleasant for a couple of hours while we played. She'd check in when she returned, and the guys would ask if she'd won or not.

About an hour and a half after we started playing, one of our smoke alarms started chirping. I did a quick inspection and determined the defective alarm was upstairs, so we played on. We wrapped up at 10:00 as planned. Ruth had said she'd be home by 8:00, so I was concerned.

I tried calling her cell phone as I set out to change the batteries. She didn't answer.

The smoke alarms speak while you're servicing them. "Bad

batteries" repeated as I replaced them. I recall thinking I'd just replaced them two weeks prior because I was preparing the condo for our trip south. I pulled the batteries, put in the new, and walked across the room to toss the old in the trash. That's when I looked up and saw a red light in the front door's side window. As soon as I saw the light, the doorbell sounded. That moment was the beginning of the rest of my life.

I was awake for most of the rest of the night. When I did try to sleep, I tossed and turned, and couldn't get the "bad batteries" out of my thoughts. I retrieved them from the trash with an eye on testing them in the morning. It took another day to determine the batteries were indeed "good."

There's no doubt in my mind that Ruth triggered the alarm. It sounded through the hours I played cards and went silent when I changed the batteries. Less than two minutes later, the officers were at my door.

Ruth and I spoke often about what's next. We weren't religious people, but I'd say we were spiritual. We both believed that spirits have visited us throughout our years together. Ruth's dad, Lou, visited us numerous times. We both could feel his presence.

On Thursday, I had the opportunity to "Facetime" with Michael's wife, Kate, who stayed in California to care for young Jackson. About ten minutes before I made the call, Michael set our Roomba free to sweep the floor. It traveled back and forth gathering up crumbs we adults were too lazy to sweep up ourselves.

While I was sharing the story of the smoke alarm, the Roomba started to beep. It was stuck in a corner, unable to free itself. I'm positive Ruth guided it to the corner to set off another alarm. She wanted Kate and Jackson to know she was thinking of them.

I don't believe in heaven or hell, but I honor the beliefs of those who do. I don't believe there's one right way, and that's why I have trouble with the concept of organized religion. I'll share more about that down the road.

Now that Ruth's moved on, one thing is perfectly clear; there's something more, and she wanted me to know.

## Chapter 49

## The Stain

Several years ago, when our three children and their spouses were celebrating somebody's something somewhere, one of them allowed themselves to be drink to "excess." As a result, his or her behavior changed. The resulting misbehavior was cause for some concern. The "over-served" individual was singled out and told they were a "stain on the family crest." Later, Elizabeth purchased a gold-colored vest from Goodwill to signify the designation. The vest was presented to "the stain."

At a second gathering some number of months later, a second violator was identified, and the vest became a traveling trophy. It was determined that all future violators would carry "the stain," and thus, hold the designation until another stain on the family crest reared his or her ugly head. The tradition has carried on for about a dozen years.

During a family discussion we determined that since we were taking the time to signal out questionable conduct, we should, in turn, recognize exceptionally positive behavior. Outstanding behavior would be awarded "the golden monkey." Each of us sought a fitting symbol to accompany the new designation. After an exhaustive search over several months that took us to dozens of exotic locations, we found the perfect symbol. It's a three-inch golden monkey statue adorned with dozens of precious stones. It's beautiful and a fitting symbol of this prestigious award.

We determined the two awards should not be awarded willy-nilly. The designation could only be made if six of the eight adults gathered. If the assembled group determined someone was worthy of the designation, a vote would be taken. We would identify a *Golden Monkey* whenever all eight adults were present but hoped a stain could be avoided. *Golden Monkey* designations would be made through a secret ballot, while stains would be made by public acclamation. I privately hoped that public shaming would lead to improved judgment. That has been the case.

Our oldest son, David, is the current holder of the *Golden Monkey*. He received the award at a gathering at his cottage in northern Michigan a couple summers ago. That was PC – Prior to Covid.

The last time the stain was awarded was about six years ago in Flagstaff, Arizona. Elizabeth and Sutton hosted the family for Thanksgiving weekend. Prior to everyone's arrival, their dog, Jonesy, ate a complete package of raw dinner rolls. We humans ate our dinner without them. Later, he devoured an entire pecan pie that Sutton had placed well outside his reach. Unfortunately, where there's a will there's a way, and Jonesy had the will. The entire group agreed he was "the stain."

"The Stain" and Golden Monkey will be up for grabs when we gather for our fiftieth wedding anniversary next month. I know the Golden Monkey will be awarded. I pray "the stain" doesn't raise its ugly head.

Update: We did indeed avoid the stain during our anniversary celebration. Ruth was awarded the Golden Monkey. It sits on the mantle above our fireplace in Michigan. Following her death, the kids decided it should be retired. No one can compete with her.

# Chapter 50

## 51 Years and Sixteen Days

The last few weeks have been tough. As I make my list of things I'm thankful for this Thanksgiving, they take on a different vibe. Losing Ruth is the hardest thing I've ever dealt with. There are no manuals on how to handle grief. You deal with each moment, not each day. They're all different.

Some may say it's trite to be thankful for your family, but I am. David, Elizabeth, and Michael are wonderful people. They're not flawless, but they're making their mark on the world. We're all better off because of who they are and the things they're accomplishing.

They've married well, and Lindsay, Sutton and Kate are perfect partners. Each couple has had their share of challenges, but like Ruth and me, they keep moving forward. That's all anyone can ask. They complement one another.

Our grandchildren, Brady, Eva and young Jackson James, are special too. They are unique, making their way on their own terms. Brady thrives athletically. Eva excels at helping others. And young Jackson, while still too young to determine his own path, likes everyone he meets and welcomes them into his life. All three are good kids, doing the best they can do during a challenging time.

My sisters, Sharron and Jackie, and Ruth's sister, Kathy, have been supportive and are dealing with Ruth's loss in their own way. My nieces have offered their support as well. I appreciate it all.

Ruth and I spoke traditional vows when we eloped on September 11, 1971. She cried, and I laughed, as we repeated each one. Neither one of us knew what the future held, but we were committed to working together. We struggled on some days, and celebrated others. We each did the best we could.

When we spoke the words, "Till death do you part," we had our eyes on the future. The future is now. I'm thankful this day, and every day, for the fifty-one years and sixteen days we shared.

## Chapter 51

### 3:16

The last time I heard from Ruth was through a text the afternoon of her accident. She made the trip to the Mt. Pleasant casino on "gas card" giveaway days. She gave the cards to our grandson, Brady. Before heading to the casino, she played a domino game called Mexican Train with several ladies at the Tullymore Country Club.

Her last text read as follows: Standing in line to get my gas card. Played Mexican train today and won 5 out of 6 games...go figure...no money just the thrill of the win.

I shared the text with Elizabeth a few days later. She asked what time Ruth sent it. It was 3:16. BZ's eyes widened as she said, "That was our original address on Grand Point Drive." Indeed, it was. 316 Grand Point Drive was where Ruth and I moved when I took the job in Addison. David was two and a half, Elizabeth six months, and Michael was just a twinkle in his father's eye.

Ruth and I spent forty-three years there. Consumers Energy changed the neighborhood house numbers as the area grew and a larger span of numbers was required. We went from 316 to 3160 and ultimately, 15176.

I shared the story with my friend, Gary, the week before I headed to Florida. Gary had considered becoming a priest early in life, so he said, "I wonder what Bible verse 3:16 is. John is the most popular book."

I looked up John 3:16 and discovered I knew it. "For God so loved the world, that he gave his only begotten Son, that whosoever believeth in him should not perish, but have everlasting life." It's the most popular verse in the Bible.

My spiritual side was open to considering that Ruth's text at 3:16, being the same as our house address, and the most popular Bible verse might all be connected. It was too much of a coincidence to ignore. And then, there's this.

My mom purchased a Mother's Day gift for Ruth in 1999. She wrote an inscription. *Mother's Day 1999 Hope you enjoy writing in this journal. Love Mom and Dad* My dad died several weeks later, on June 27th.

I found the journal the other day while going through a basket of Mother's Day and birthday cards Ruth had received and saved. There are about fifteen entries written by Ruth. I'm going to share them in a series of blogs I'll call *In Her Own Words*.

The first page of the journal is called: Personal Portrait. The "portrait" was a summary of her family. It held important dates like birthdays for her and her sisters, our three children, our wedding anniversary, and a list of "favorites." Listed among her favorites were: Flower – Peony and Lilac, Perfume – Knowing, Color – Red, Dessert – Chocolate Anything, Vacation Spot – Myrtle Beach, Sport – Basketball, Food – Italian, and Bible Verse – John 3:16.

These are the facts. 316 was our house number when we moved to Addison in 1977. It was also the time she sent me her final text on September 27th. John 3:16 is the most popular verse in the Bible, and in 1999, Ruth wrote it was her favorite Bible verse.

Perhaps it's all just a great coincidence, but perhaps it's not.

## Chapter 52

## The Worst Thing

Ruth and my first look at death as a married couple took place on April 30, 1979. I got a call at work in Addison from Ruth's Aunt Casey. She told me Ruth's dad, Lou, had a heart attack. Lou was sixty-five. Ruth and I were thirty-two. David was four, Elizabeth two, and Michael nine months.

I called my mom to ask her to come from Royal Oak to pick up David and Elizabeth to care for them for the next several days. Then I called the superintendent's wife, Carolyn, to ask her to watch the two until my mom arrived. We'd take Michael with us to Plainwell. I had the plan in place before I drove home to speak with Ruth. It was the most devastating news I ever shared with her. Lou thought Ruth hung the moon and she felt the same about her dad.

Among Ruth's attributes was the fact she gave Lou two grandsons. He had three daughters of his own, and two granddaughters from Ruth's older sister, Shirley, but David was the first boy. Lou liked boys, and he loved David. Perhaps most important, David loved Lou.

The week we spent in Plainwell was very somber. After the first night together, we took Michael to spend a couple of days with his Grandpa Jack and Grandma Em Walker.

Everyone was shocked by Lou's passing. He'd never been sick and was a man's man. He's the only man who I feared. I knew if I ever wronged his daughter, there'd be hell to pay.

Near the end of the week, my mom and dad brought David and Elizabeth to Kalamazoo. We all met up at Jack and Emma's. We shed some tears and shared stories, doing our best to support one another. The kids were too young to understand what was happening with the adults.

The task of speaking with David about his grandfather fell to me. We went off by ourselves and sat face to face. I don't recall the words I used, but in the end, I said something like, "God took Grandpa to heaven to live with him. He won't be with us anymore." Then David said, "I'm gonna punch God right in the nose." That's probably the worst thing a four-year-old could do.

With Ruth's passing, this seventy-five-year-old feels the same.

# Chapter 53

# My New Seating Chart

The story below was among my first blog posts. With Ruth's passing, I've updated it a bit. It's a long read, but worth a second look.

*Many people – perhaps most around the world – never have the chance to share a meal at a table with their family. I've been lucky to have four dinner tables in my life.*

*My first table was with my Mom and Dad. My sister Sharron joined us in 1950, and Jackie arrived in 1954. The table had a Formica top with a leaf that you could add for company. What I remember most about the experience is we all ate together. While that wasn't always possible because of my father's long work hours, the kids and Mom were always together at the table. Dad was there most of the time. He made up for lost dinners by making breakfast on the weekends for everyone.*

*We had an undocumented seating chart. I sat next to the wall and Sharron sat to my left. Mom sat directly across from me. Jackie's* highchair (and eventually regular chair) was to the right of Mom's. Dad sat at the end between Sharron and Jackie. My Grandma Tebo joined us for a couple of years after my Grandpa Tebo passed. The chart was rearranged during those years, but the process of sharing time remained the same.

I don't remember what we talked about, but I know we talked. We had a set of finger puppets that Dad often brought out to speak with the girls after we finished eating. The puppets whistled rather than spoke, but everyone knew what they were saying. It was a high-pitched through the teeth whistle with great expression. The puppets offered advice, often asked questions, and frequently reminded Sharron to finish her dinner.

I very distinctly remember (and I'm not proud to share this) one conversation that went awry for me.

I had the habit of saying, "tough rocks" to my sister, Sharron, whenever she would complain about anything. I may have offered the two words even if she wasn't complaining. I was the cool older brother, and she needed my words of wisdom. I was about eleven when I switched it up a bit and threw this out to her at the dinner table.

Me: "Tough titty said the kitty but the milk's still good."
Mom: "Where did you hear that?"
Me: "I don't know."
Mom: "Don't ever say that again."
So, I didn't.

My second shared table was in college. Gary, Jim, and I lived together in apartments for the final two-plus years of our college education. An assortment of guys joined us to complete the foursome and share the rent, but the three of us were the constant amigos.

The summer between our second and third years of college, we met to discuss our plan to move out of the dorm and into an apartment. We decided to kick in $15.00 a week to purchase our food, cleaning supplies, etc. Jim became our cook, Gary did the dishes, and I cleaned the place. As chief cook, the shopping duties and meal scheduling fell upon Jim.

*We offered our input to the meal schedule, but Jim took on the major duties.*

*Pot pies and BLTs were on the menu every week. You could have any flavor of pie you wished, and we always had two each. We were growing boys.*

*The BLTs were not your momma's BLTs. They were Jim's. He felt his mother had scrimped on the bacon when she made BLTs for his family. The bacon was piled high on Jim's, and they were deeeeeelicious.*

*Our dinner conversations focused on our classes, career choices, current events, upcoming parties, and girls. But mostly parties and girls.*

*My third table has been shared with Ruth in two distinct phases – with children and without. While the shape and size of our table has changed throughout the years, its purpose has always remained the same. It's the place that we've planned for our future, lived in the present, and reminisced about our past. We've laughed and cried on several occasions.*

*Our very first table was ash and an antique when we bought it. We shared it for forty-four years until we decided to ship it to Flagstaff, Arizona where Sutton and Elizabeth share it today. We've stopped in several times to visit the three of them, and look forward to our next visit. I expect that they are experiencing similar happy and sad times.*

*Ruth and I are fortunate to have two tables in our lives. One remains in Michigan where we raised three children. David had a lone seat at the table for the first two years of his life. Michael had a lone seat as well, but his was held after David and Elizabeth went off to college where I expect they ate pot pies and BLTs with their new friends. Michael moved on a year later to share similar meals with his roommates. Elizabeth never had a lone seat but that might be the subconscious reason we shipped that ash table to Arizona.*

*Another table is housed in Florida where we are experiencing new things with new people. It's our refuge to avoid the cold of Michigan's winter, and more importantly, Michigan's snow.*

*No matter where Ruth and I sit today to share our dinner, we always look forward to our children and their families sitting with us.*

*When David, Elizabeth and Michael were young, we always did our best to have dinner together. This table was the busiest. With two working parents, and three kids participating in a variety of school activities, this was sometimes a challenge. We made it work because it was important. We had a lot of "what if" conversations at our table. Ruth or I would throw out a conversation starter like, "What would you do if a stranger approached you at the bus stop?" and the discussion would progress from that point. "What would you do if one of your friends came to school without his lunch?" is another example. We discussed a vast array of topics with a variety of voice inflections.*

*The most important thing about these discussions was they were inclusive. Everyone participated. We shared our time and thoughts with each other. We did what we did because we were a family, and this was an important part of being together. We learned with, and from, each other.*

*Some of our conversations took surprising turns. Not for the kids, but for Ruth and me. I remember after more than one such dinner conversation, we'd retreat to another part of the house and ask, "Do you believe what we just talked about? I wouldn't talk to my parents about this, even today. Wow!!!"*

I still have tables in Michigan and Florida. They aren't the same as I had when I originally wrote this tale. Ruth was always on the lookout for something new, even if it was just new to the two of us. We were in a constant state of revision. New looks and new feels ruled the day.

My plans are simple. I'll maintain the status quo. I don't see any new tables in the near future. I'm still adjusting to sitting alone and relying on memories to keep me company. The biggest change is the silence.

I celebrate the fact that David, Elizabeth, and Michael have tables of their own. They've moved them from place to place, with more moves and seating arrangements on the horizon, but they are theirs with conversations of their own. I think Ruth and I provided a good model for each to adapt as they see fit. And that makes me smile.

# Chapter 54

# Losers

I had lunch the other day with three friends. After we spoke, I thought about our conversation and determined we're four losers. I don't mean that disrespectfully, but we've each lost someone in the past several months, and we share the common bond of loss.

Kathy's husband woke up one Monday morning and announced he was leaving and wanted a divorce. The declaration came out of the blue with little or no warning. The split came and the aftermath has been difficult to handle.

Paul has been married twice. He and his first wife divorced and his second died last January. She had been ill for five years and needed his support throughout. He lost her a little at a time.

Sandy's husband suffered a brain aneurism last spring. He lived for two weeks before he passed. She had some time to deal with the loss, but the hurt is just as painful.

And then, there's me. Ruth and I spoke one Tuesday morning, making plans for a trip to California where I sit today. After our conversation, she went off to do "her thing" and she never came home.

All four had a different type of loss, but they're each painful. We spoke briefly of our circumstances and made the common observation that sudden loss may be worse for the survivor but better for the one who passes. Losing someone a little at a time is hard on everyone. While I wish I would have had a "heads up" regarding Ruth, I don't know what I would have done with it. What would we have done differently? Would we have traveled more? Visited the kids more frequently? Treated one another differently? Spent our time and money more lavishly? Settled in one place to live? Been more frugal?

My dad died in 1999. My mom took him to the hospital one Saturday in September because he was dehydrated, and he never lived at home again. I sat with him for most of the following day, wondering what would happen next. He had Parkinson's disease for several years, and its grip was tightening. A few days later, the doctors determined he'd need a feeding tube and he asked me what I thought. I recall asking him if he was ready to "give up" or wanted to "keep going." He opted for the latter. That's when I said, "Then you've gotta get the tube."

He spent his last nine months in nursing homes and hospitals. I visited him every week and reconnected with the man who raised me. I had spent most of the past thirty plus years raising a family of my own and connected with my parents when it suited me. We saw each other frequently, but I'm sure not as much as they would have liked. Dad's illness, and the fact that my children had lives of their own, helped rekindle our bond. I learned new things about him, and he learned more about me. We shared our time and that's when I realized how valuable time truly is. While I knew it, I sometimes failed to follow through with the lesson learned.

Losing someone you love is a challenge no matter what the circumstances may be. We need to focus on the here and now, because none of us knows what tomorrow may bring. I understand that more now than ever. Celebrate now and take care of the people that matter most while you still have the opportunity.

# Chapter 55

# Anxiety

I'd heard the word but never really thought seriously about it until Ruth died. I didn't understand how you came to be affected by such a demon, and now I do. It just crept up. I didn't know I had it, until I did. It's not like getting a cold or the flu. If there were symptoms, I didn't recognize them. They just appeared out of nowhere.

Sure, I've been anxious over the years. My first recollection was when I went to junior high school as a seventh grader. Junior high was the blending of students from several different elementary schools. The first day of every class began the same. The teacher called the roll. Each name was rambled off in alphabetical order. Some were mispronounced and some sounded funny to the assembled students. Jim Polman became Polecat. Tebo became Tebone or Tebone steak. I hated that first day and the first day of my eighth and ninth grade years. By the time my sophomore year rolled around, the novelty subsided.

I felt anxious when I asked a girl out on a date for the first time. I'd practice what I'd say and how I'd say it. There was always a sense of relief after the ask. I never had a girl turn me down, but there were several I didn't ask because of the fear they would. They were opportunities lost.

Sheri Z sat in front of me in my senior year History of Religion class. We spoke every day and I thought she was too cute to go out with me, so I never asked. Heck, she dated guys in college, and I couldn't compete with that. The fear of getting a "no" was more than I could handle.

She asked if we could exchange "senior pictures" on the last day of class. Such an exchange included writing something on the back of the picture. Most exchanges included notes like: "Good luck at Western!", "May all your dreams come true," or "I wish you nothing but the best wherever life may take you." Sheri wrote, "I wish you would have asked me out." I never saw her again after that last day of school. Opportunity lost.

Common anxiety signs and symptoms include:

- **Feeling nervous, restless or tense**
- Having a sense of impending danger, panic or doom
- **Having an increased heart rate**
- Breathing rapidly (hyperventilation)
- **Sweating**
- Trembling
- **Feeling** weak or **tired**
- **Trouble concentrating** or thinking about anything other than the present worry
- **Having trouble sleeping**
- Experiencing gastrointestinal (GI) problems
- Having difficulty controlling worry
- Having the urge to avoid things that trigger anxiety.

I've highlighted the ones I've experienced since September 27th. I shared my symptoms with my doctor during my annual wellness visit. He offered to write a prescription, but I declined. I don't take any medications on a regular basis, and I'm not interested in starting now.

I've had two meetings with a shrink. She's not really a shrink, but rather, a licensed clinical social worker like my daughter, Elizabeth. During our first session she told me she had two questions. 1) She knew my wife had died, so she wanted to know if I could tell her what happened. 2) She wanted to know what I hoped to gain from our time together.

Once I began, I verbal vomited for an hour straight. I had lots to say and a willing listener. I shared a multitude of thoughts and spoke briefly about being anxious. I described my feelings, and she told me it was normal, particularly so after experiencing such a loss. That didn't make me feel any better, but at least I knew I was normal. I'll take normal even if it feels broken. She also told me there's no timeline for feeling less anxious.

I've learned anxiety and grief are emotional buddies. They hang out together and tend to travel as a pair. When one shows up, the other is close by. I don't care for either one, but we're learning to live together. One day at a time, they say. Most days are good. The challenge comes most often when I see, or speak, with an old friend for the first time. I'm often asked what happened and the retelling is a challenge. It's funny though, when I'm done, I feel better. It's like I've unloaded a bit of my burden. Writing helps too. I unload a bit more and sort things out.

When people ask how I'm doing, my reply is simple. "I'm doing the best I can today." That's all I can do.

# Chapter 56

# Thank You, Obadiah

I have a Facebook friend, Obadiah, who posted a cartoon a few days ago. It was a visual representation of how people handle problems. Two men, stuck in the same position, take two different paths. One sits and ponders his misfortune, while the other tries to dig his way out, working to improve his lot in life. It reminded me of me. Sometimes I'm a sitter and sometimes I'm a digger. I need to be a digger every day.

When the kids were growing up, Ruth preached the concept of choices. She contended that we all have them and the choices we make determine our lot in life. In their youth, they grew tired of her words. They knew what she was going to say before she said it. With age comes wisdom, and somewhere along the way, they decided she was right. I knew it all along.

After Ruth's accident, I plowed through a myriad of business issues. I updated financial accounts, closed some, opened new ones, moved money, had my attorney update my legal documents, and making sure things were in order for my kids. That part of my life is in good shape. The personal issues need attention.

I promised myself I'd take things slowly. I wouldn't make any quick decisions for fear of making poor ones. I decided maintaining the status quo was better than moving too quickly. Now, I think standing still may be just as bad.

I reconnected with my shrink last week and discussed my current status. We've only met three times; once in November, once in December, and then last week. The best part of discussing issues with her is I unload everything I'm thinking, and she passes no judgment. She asks questions as needed but lets me speak my peace. The practical side of me knows she's getting paid to listen, so I unload. I leave some of my burdens with her and walk away feeling a bit better.

For me, it's kind of like getting a massage for my brain. I don't get many full body massages, but when I do, I tell my massage therapist to go full bore. I don't want him to play paddycake paddycake with my muscles. Don't hold back. I want to know that I was there when I leave. That's how my relationship with my shrink is developing.

As last week's session drew to a close, I told my shrink of Obadiah's Facebook message. She listened attentively and asked why it spoke to me. When I finished my explanation, she asked if I'd ever heard of "An Autobiography in Five Chapters." I said, "No," and her fingers danced across her cell phone in search of it. She read it to me. I think Obadiah's Facebook post and Portia Nelson's poem have a lot in common.

"An Autobiography in Five Chapters"
by Portia Nelson

*Chapter One*
I walk down the street.
There is a deep hole in the sidewalk.
I fall in. I am lost.... I am helpless.
It isn't my fault.
It takes forever to find a way out.

*Chapter Two*
I walk down the same street.
There is a deep hole in the sidewalk.
I pretend I don't see it. I fall in again.
I can't believe I am in the same place.
But it isn't my fault.
It still takes a long time to get out.

*Chapter Three*
I walk down the same street.
There is a deep hole in the sidewalk.
I see it is there.
I fall in.... it's a habit... but my eyes are open.
I know where I am. It is my fault.
I get out immediately.

*Chapter Four*
I walk down the same street.
There is a deep hole in the sidewalk.
I walk around it.

*Chapter Five*
I walk down a different street.


I'm living in Chapter Three today. I'm not sure how or when I arrived, but I recognize my predicament. If it's going to change, I have to change it. Doing the same thing day after day isn't working for me. If I want to walk around the hole or take a different street, I have to keep digging like the man in Obadiah's Facebook cartoon.

## Chapter 57

## Tears

The first time I saw my father cry was December of 1955. Our family had been out Christmas shopping and visiting Santa Claus. We'd just walked in the door when Dad headed to the hallway. I didn't hear the phone ring, but Dad came back through the living room after a short phone conversation and said, "Pa died today." He walked out to the front porch to be alone, and I saw him wipe his eyes.

Grandpa Tebo had fallen and broken his hip. He'd been in the hospital about two weeks and developed pneumonia. That's what killed him.

A few days later, I saw Dad cry again. We were gathered in the funeral home, and he walked into the single stall restroom tucked under a set of stairs. He wanted to be alone. I saw him reach for his handkerchief and wipe his eyes as he closed the door behind him. I thought to myself, "he doesn't want anyone to see." I was eight years old, had cried plenty of times myself, but this was the first time I saw someone cry because they were sad. It's a different kind of cry. It starts in your soul and eases its way out.

I didn't see him cry again for decades. I know he did. I just didn't see him. The tears I did see came much later in life and were triggered by an assortment of emotions. Sadness was high on the list. He was a happy man, easy to get along with, and everyone liked him. He became sad when he thought about the suffering of others. We call that empathy.

I've had my share of tears lately. They come less often as the months and weeks have passed. My tears are the "come from your soul" type. They ease out while listening to music on the car radio, when I read entries from Ruth's journals or find notes she's written, and sometimes when I write.

I joined a writer's group in The Villages, and each member has the opportunity to read a story they've written. We read to the group, and the assembled members critique each piece. I've learned to avoid stories that mention Ruth, as more often than not, my words get caught in my throat as I try to avoid the accompanying tears. I take a deep breath, try to calm my nerves, but I just choke on the words.

I have friends that share my grief. I spent part of the weekend with several. We talked about our families and shared both happy and troublesome news. All families have stories to share, but we don't always have someone we trust to share them with. Luckily, I do.

I did find myself choking back tears a time or two while talking about Ruth, but that's ok. They understand and have choked on tears of their own.

For those who may be concerned about my frankness, don't be. Tears, like laughter, are a part of life. We hold them both in our soul, and they come out as needed. They make us human, and without one, the other might not be so special.

## Chapter 58

## Spaghetti and Applesauce

Ruth was a "waste not, want not" type girl. She saved a lot of things and wasted few. She repurposed objects and made the old new. She had a knack for it. We visited hundreds of craft shows, and more often than not, she said, "I can make that." Sometimes she did. Sometimes she didn't.

I have loads of bubble wrap, Christmas wrapping, and tissue paper. She had at least one drawer full in each house. We have recycled Christmas boxes dating back to the years all three kids lived at home. They save a lot of time wrapping and writing gift cards. I used a couple this year for David and his crew. I'm still stumbling upon the treasures she saved in Florida. There will be tons more when I get back to Michigan in May.

The kids and I will be going through a dozen tubs of Christmas decorations Ruth saved. She's got a ton of special tree ornaments and several collectible Santa Claus dolls stored for safe keeping. There's a good chance you'll see some on eBay this summer.

Every time we moved from Florida to Michigan, or Michigan to Florida, she took several items from the refrigerator and put them in the freezer. Her process ensured the food would still be good when we returned six months later. Open cans of coffee, cartons of milk, strawberries, blueberries, whole bananas, and pineapple chunks all found their way to the freezer. She thought a full freezer ran more economically. We saved food and money through her frugal efforts.

When I arrived in Florida last November, I stumbled upon two saved treasures. There was a large container of homemade spaghetti with meat sauce and a small one with handcrafted applesauce. The container of spaghetti was large, so she must have squirreled it away shortly after making it. We probably were invited out for dinner on the night she made it. Rather than waste a good time with friends, she saved it for another day.

The applesauce looked like it had been made with two or three apples. Rather than have them go to waste when we headed north, she made the sauce and froze it for the following fall. She just didn't make it back down to share with me.

I let the treasures stay frozen until last week. I ate a few bites of the applesauce each day for several days. I consumed the spaghetti in the same fashion. I ate both sparingly, as I knew when they were gone, a small part of her would disappear as well.

It's the simple things I miss most.

# Chapter 59

# My Elephant

If you've read my blogs, you know my daughter, Elizabeth, wrote and published a children's book called *The Elephant on Aaron's Chest*. It came out last February.

It had taken several years to finish, but great things can't be rushed. Great takes time.

We had a wonderful celebration in California when the book rolled out. David flew in from Michigan. Ruth and I, as well as Ruth's sister, Kathy, flew in from Florida. Michael, Kate, and young Jackson James all attended. The book launch was a magnificent reason for us to be together. We've tried to get together once or twice a year since my "California kids" moved west, but Covid put a damper on us.

The book is about depression, isolation, anxiety, loss, and a dozen other similar feelings. Aaron is a young boy dealing with feelings of despair. He's troubled, finding it difficult to do the things he once enjoyed. He attempts to rid himself of his elephant in a variety of ways, but he struggles.

Since Ruth's death four weeks ago, grief has become my elephant. He climbs on most evenings and settles in for a few hours.

Evening was the time we shared most, as our days were filled with our own interests.

Like Aaron, I'll learn to accept my elephant, but now it's tough. I take comfort in knowing her final summer was one of her best. She made new friends, engaged in new activities, and applied her finishing touches on our Tullymore condo. She said, "It's perfect and I love it here," just a week prior to her accident.

All three kids visited us and spent some one-on-one time with Ruth. She'd traveled to California to see Elizabeth and Sutton's new home, and spent a couple of days with Jackson, Mike, and Kate. She reveled in every minute as it was truly a special summer.

I've learned a ton over the past four weeks. The biggest lesson is no matter how much you plan for "what's next" you can never be sure, so do the things you love when you have the opportunity. You don't know when you'll have your last chance.

When I started this blog, my categories were Family, Career Lessons, Childhood Memories, Current Events, and Random Thoughts. With her passing, I've added a new one— Ruth. Elizabeth noted that I've seldom written just about Ruth over these past five blog years. That'll change now.

## Chapter 60

## Widower

When I was a kid, the first widow I learned about was a spider. I knew black widows could be deadly, and for several months I thought we had one living in our fruit cellar. The fruit cellar was the former coal bin of our house at 500 N. Edgeworth. It was a repurposed spot in our basement. Dad built shelves to store the jars of fruit and the fresh tomatoes he bought from Detroit's Eastern Market for Mom to can. It also held the grape and raspberry jelly she made from the fruit in our backyard.

Dad sent one of us three kids to the cellar to retrieve a jar of jelly when we ran low in the kitchen. The chosen child got to select which flavor jelly to retrieve. It was quite an honor. Once I saw the spider, I deferred to the girls. We had two, and if one of them was bitten and died, we still had a spare. At least that's how this older brother looked at the situation. It wasn't until I took junior high science that I determined it wasn't a black widow at all, because it didn't have the red hourglass marking on its underside. I skipped a lot of opportunities to select the jelly for nothing.

I learned about human widows and widowers when my grandparents died. When Grandpa Tebo died in 1955, Grandma

Tebo became a widow. Three years later, Grandpa Barner became a widower when Grandma Barner died. I didn't think much about either word until I became one myself.

I was filling out a membership form at a local gym a couple of weeks ago, and when I came to the part that referenced marital status, I checked the widower box. It wasn't an automatic check like so many of the yes and no questions we're asked on such documents. It was a take a deep breath and a pause before answering type response. I went to a new dentist last week and was confronted with the same question. I took the same pause before answering.

"Widow," "widower," and "widowed" are three terms no one wants to have applied to themselves, as they imply the loss of a spouse. I never thought about it before, but Ruth and I both signed up for the possibility when we recited our "until death do you part" vows. We all do if we take the vows seriously.

Three dozen years ago, one of my mom's elderly aunts died in Bowling Green, Kentucky. Mom drove to Kentucky to attend the funeral with her father and his second wife, Virginia. It was a brief trip lasting only a couple of days. She returned home the afternoon of the funeral. By the time she'd made the seven-hour drive home, her uncle had died. The passing of his wife was too much for him to handle, so he just gave up.

I've been both sad and mad since Ruth's passing, so I understand sadness and anger. I don't care for either one, but I'm learning to live with the feelings when they creep in. Logical me believes I have two choices; move forward or give up. Moving forward and learning to live with loss is the path I'm on. While some days are more challenging than others, I still have things I want to do and places I'd like to see. The tough part will be figuring out if I do them alone or with someone new.

I've been told I should wait a year until I make any major changes. I'm good with that advice. If there's a manual about being a widower, I've not seen it. I have a fellow widower living across the street from my Florida home. He invited me to talk with him anytime I feel the need. He told me he didn't want me to "do anything stupid." I assured him I wouldn't.

Living in Florida is different than living in Michigan. Ruth and I had been living in our new condo for less than two years. We were really just getting to know the lay of the land when she had her accident. We had each other to share our time and make plans with. The only couple friends we had moved away shortly after Ruth's accident. When I head north in May, I'll need to establish a new support system. If I decide to spend more time in Florida, I need to expand my circle of friends because most of my current Florida friends are snowbirds like me.

There are plenty of opportunities to make friends in both locations. The challenge is to make the first move, even if it's wrong. I've always encouraged the people I worked with, and later my children, to be risk takers. Stepping out of one's comfort zone is tough, but in my case, it's a necessity if I'm going to keep on keepin' on.

I've been a widower for four months and two days, so I'm early in the process. If you see or hear of me doing things you don't understand, please be patient. I've got to figure this out on my own, however, if I seek your advice, please give it to me straight as I'm too old to make too many mistakes.

## Chapter 61

## A Better Way

Just before heading south last October, our condo association held an open house at one of the condo owners' homes. About eighty people were invited, an RSVP was requested, and after giving it some thought, I accepted the invitation. The party planner said she was happy I was attending. On the surface I took her reply to mean she was happy I was attending even though Ruth could not. I assumed everyone in the association knew of Ruth's accident, since the country club we're associated with had sent her obituary to the membership.

I arrived at the designated time and was welcomed with a "We're so happy you made it." The greeting reinforced my belief that everyone knew of Ruth's passing.

About an hour after it began, a group of ladies inquired about my wife. "Where's your wife?" was the question asked. The lady with the question was very proud of herself. She looked like she was offering up "the challenge question of the day" on behalf of the assembled group. I took a deep breath, looked at the floor, gathered myself, stood erect, and told them she'd been killed in a car accident a month earlier. They were all apologetic and offered words of condolence. The asker said, "I wish I'd never asked." Me too.

I attended a social gathering in Florida a couple of days ago. A man that I'd met a year or so ago asked where my wife was. After five months my response is easier to say. "She died in September. She had a heart attack while driving, crashed her car, and died." He offered his condolences and our conversation drifted off to more conventional topics.

Neither the October lady nor last weekend's man meant any harm. They both caused me to take pause in what would normally be just another day. I wasn't happy I was asked such a question and wondered privately if I've ever asked it myself. It's a perfectly normal question until you have an answer like mine.

Since becoming a widower, I've wondered how people in my shoes share such news. I still wear my wedding ring and haven't given any serious thought to removing it. When Ruth and I put our rings on, she told me to "never take it off." I expect there are hundreds of thousands, perhaps millions, of people in the same boat. The decision to seek new companionship is one that each one of us will make at some point. We will or we won't.

I have a poker friend whose wife died a few months prior to Ruth. He's said that he'd like to go out for lunch or dinner, or perhaps a movie or play, with someone new. "It would be nice to have a new companion." The challenge is knowing who's available. Unless you have inside information, you can't really know. We've agreed that availability must supersede such an ask.

When you're young, you take your chances. Rejection is a part of the process. At almost seventy-six, if there's a manual on establishing new relationships, I'd like to read it. My poker friend and I are wondering how to begin anew even if we're not ready to move forward. We'd like to be prepared for when we are. There must be a better way than just guessing.

# Chapter 62

## $15

Brady plans to go to Grand Rapids Community College next fall. He was recruited to play on the basketball team with a promise that the coach would help get him to the "next level." We've discussed potential career paths, but right now he, like thousands of other graduates across the country, isn't committed to one. Community College is a good path. He'll be able to improve his athletic skills while taking a cost effective first step through higher education.

The only problem with GRCC is there is no on campus housing options. He needs to commute from home or get an apartment. Getting an apartment is everyone's number one priority. He wants one, his parents want him to get one, and I think it's a great idea. Housing is probably going to cost more than his tuition. A couple weeks ago he said his first choice was a single studio apartment. When I asked him why he preferred to live alone he said, "I don't want anyone telling me what to do."

I went on to say, "When you're living on your own, your roommate is not going to tell you what to do. If he, or she, does you can choose to ignore the suggestion or tell them to take a leap at a flying donut. That's part of the beauty of living on your own. You're responsible for yourself."

I went a step further and offered myself as a roommate. I'm probably not his first choice but there are a lot of upsides to the two of us living together.

1. We're both single.
2. I have a lot of stuff I can bring to the apartment. I own duplicates of several items, including furniture.
3. I'll be commuting from Florida most of the winter, so I won't be around much. He'll practically be living alone.
4. I have no interest in "telling him what to do."
5. While I'm not ready to start dating, when I am, I can scout out granddaughters for him and he can scout out grandmothers for me. It's a win-win.
6. I've lived the college life myself, so I can pass on words of wisdom from time to time.
7. I've got a lot of extra ties, so I can teach him the old "tie on the doorknob" signage trick.
8. I'll insist on a two-bedroom apartment, so when I'm out of town, he'll have room for buddies to spend a night or two.
9. I'm a good cook, and I prefer cooking for two.
10. I'm pretty good at picking up after myself. He could learn a lesson or two from me, because they'll be no moms to pick up after us.

My only concern about the arrangement is decor. Neither one of us is very good at decorating. Sure, he's got a lot of posters in his room. We could move them. I've certainly got things that could be repurposed in any apartment we might share. But if we're really going to do this, we've got to establish our own style, and do it on a budget. Ruth taught me that.

So, here's my idea. We go with one statement piece in the main living area. We don't want a lot of doodads and whatnots. They've got to be dusted, and of all the homemaking skills I have, dusting is dead last. And to tell you the truth, I don't think Brady's ever dusted.

Ruth purchased a large 60 by 45-inch picture for each of our homes. We have a water scene in our Michigan condo and a beach boardwalk picture in our Florida home. You can't miss them.

I think we should blow up a picture of Brady and me from back in the day. I'd gladly make the investment. I have a photo of me holding him as a baby. I was fifty-eight at the time and he was six months. It would make a great statement piece and help us strike up some conversations with any ladies that might drop by.

Once we decorate the place, we'll need to develop a household budget.

Shortly after I graduated from high school my parents started charging me $15 a week for room and board. The collections began around the first of July in 1965. I had a job, so they charged me what they thought was a reasonable fee.

My living conditions didn't change. I still had my own room, Mom did my laundry, and I ate what I wanted whenever I wanted. The payments stopped when I went off to college but resumed each summer when I came back home. It was my first lesson on being independent. The gravy train stopped. I had to pay my own way.

I don't know if my sisters shared the same experience, but paying my fair share was part of my deal. I also had to pay my car insurance and gas for my parent's cars. I didn't have my own until just prior to my junior year of college.

Brady's mom and dad have been more generous. He's got his own car. They cover most, if not all, of the associated expenses, and he wants for very little. He's had an extra bacon and guacamole appetite but a McDonald's Value meal personal income stream. That's all about to change.

To be fair, he's had a job the last few summers. This year he's working at a marina, and as I understand it, doing quite well. This year though, he's learning to save. He'll have expenses in college with no concrete income stream.

I shared my first college apartment with three other guys. I lived with Gary and Jim for two years. Dan, Don (AKA Fuzzy), Ash, and Jeff rotated through as our fourth. We chipped in $15.00 a week for food and common supplies like toilet paper, cleaning compounds, and dish detergent. We learned to live on a budget. We ate well while being cost conscious. We supplied our own personal needs but shared our common expenses.

If Brady and I chipped in $15.00 a week for food, we'd starve. A loaf of bread cost twenty cents when I was in college. We could get three pounds of hamburger for less than a dollar. We ate pot pies once a week. We each had two and they cost about twenty-three cents apiece.

If we choose to live on a similar budget, we'll have to pay $135 each. I'm living on a fixed income, but I can handle it. I'm not sure Brady can.

I think David and Lindsay would allow us to do our laundry at their house. It's only about a half hour from campus. If we timed it right, we'd probably get a free lunch or dinner out of the deal. We might even be able to cob a roll, or two, of toilet paper. That would save us a few dollars, and they might enjoy the visit.

But in the long run, you've got to pay "the man." Responsible people pay their own way. It's not easy, and it's certainly not fun, but independence comes with a cost. If he does a good job, as I know he will, Brady will have the opportunity to provide for his own family one day. He's just getting started.

If we decide not to become roommates, I'm sure he'll find another. He's a handsome young man with a magnetic personality. That will open a lot of doors for him, but in the end, it's hard work that will ensure his success. Should he stumble, I can toss him a few bucks, and Nana will always have his back.

## Chapter 63

## Life Lessons

I wrote a blog about my friend, Ed, as he turned 101 back in November of 2018. Although I didn't ask him, I speculated that he might offer up this list of guiding principles as his secret to his longevity.

1. Love. Share your time on earth. You don't have to marry, but have someone to share your time, encourage your goals, listen to your thoughts, and set you straight when you veer off path.
2. Take care of yourself. Value your health. Avoid excess.
3. Believe in something bigger than yourself. Be religious if that's a path you choose, but in any case, make sure that you know that there is something more important than each of us, alone.
4. Work. Be engaged in something that helps you find purpose. If your first choice doesn't work out, find another. Each of us needs to have a reason to get up each morning. Make sure that you have something to look forward to doing each day.

5. Hang with people younger than you at least some of the time. Share your experience. Don't be afraid to share your failures as well as your triumphs.
6. Laugh. Belly laughs are preferred.
7. Belong. Be an active part of a community. It may be church, your neighbors, people at work, your school, a team, a club or your family. Each of us needs to engage with others that share a common bond.
8. Play. Have fun and share your experience with others.
9. Sing and dance even if you only sing in the shower and tap your foot to music while sitting in a chair. It's good for the soul.
10. Don't keep score. If someone does you wrong, move on. Be the bigger man (or woman). You'll waste a lot of time that you could be loving, caring, believing, working, hanging, laughing, belonging, playing, singing and dancing.

I may have borrowed the list from someone else, I don't recall. I do believe it's a good list.

When I look at my life, I think I've excelled at number four but may have focused on work at the expense of others on the list. Numbers two and ten are my weaknesses. Since Ruth's passing, I've learned a bit more about number three. Numbers five and eight are important to me. I love being with my kids and now I have the opportunity to hang with my grandchildren. Seven is about sharing your time and I need to do more of that. Six and nine go hand in hand. Number one is most important to me. In that regard, I've been very lucky.

I think each of us should have a set of guiding principles. Use this one or develop your own. Perhaps the Ten Commandments, or another set of religious tenets, work best for you. No matter how you choose to live your life, do it with purpose.

## Chapter 64

## The Red Plate

If you're a long-time blog reader, or one of our many friends, you know that Ruth and I eloped. Once we were married, our parents planned after-the-fact receptions. The Van Bruggens held a low-key cake and coffee gathering in their home in Plainwell, and my parents threw an all-out Detroit style bash. There was a band, a ton of food, drinking and dancing.

Ruth and I registered for gifts like any other couple. We had the advantage of having acquired a few things as single adults, but setting up a home was a different story. We anticipated receiving gifts in Plainwell and cash in Detroit. That's how the two sides of the state traditionally supported married couples.

We registered together. I deferred to Ruth on most matters but stuck to my guns when it came to bedding: sheets, pillowcases, bedspreads, and blankets. I wanted nothing to do with flowers. I preferred solid colors or stripes. She honored my request and we registered accordingly. Unfortunately, the gift purchasers went freelance on us and we got sets of flower sheets. We used them because we had a waste not, want not attitude. I suppose we could have returned or regifted them but if the original purchasers showed up, we wanted concrete evidence that we'd put their gift to good use.

Our longest discussion focused on china. We wanted a formal set of dishes for dinner parties and holidays. We agreed that our everyday dishes should be white, but a china pattern was a different story. Again, I wanted nothing to do with flowers, so we settled on a pattern that was acceptable to both. It had a blue accent and was flower-free. Over time, we built a service for twelve with serving platters, assorted sized bowls, dessert plates, cups and saucers, and a sugar and creamer set. What we didn't get as wedding gifts, Ruth received as birthday and Christmas gifts from her mom and mine.

Our sterling silver goal was eight sets. Each set included salad and dinner forks, a teaspoon, and a knife. Twelve sets of sterling silver was too lofty a goal. It took a couple years, but we acquired that as well. The serving pieces that accompanied the silver cost $100 each and this was 1971.

We registered for, and received, a dozen crystal glasses. They cost $5.00 during a time when you could go to the "dime store" and purchase two glasses for twenty-five cents. Cha-ching.

During our fifty-one years and sixteen days, I'd estimate we used our china a hundred times. We didn't use it every year, but every once in a while, Ruth would pull them out wondering what we were saving them for. We used it for family dinners, a couple of dinner parties we held before the kids were born, and sometimes just the two of us. We used the crystal glasses in a similar fashion.

The silver is a different story. While it's true we kept it in a case under the living room couch when the kids were little, we pulled it out and used it on a regular basis. It was available every day.

Yesterday, while I was looking for something else, I found our single red plate. Ruth bought it when the kids were young. She set the red plate when David, Elizabeth, or Michael had a birthday. She served each one of them on the red plate when they accomplished something noteworthy. It was special. She and I got to use it a couple of times.

I don't recall the last time we pulled it out. We probably used it for Brady and Eva a time or two. If not, I will.

I've set the red plate at the table and I'm going to leave it there. It's a bit worn, but that just shows how special it is. I've added the appropriate silver on either side. I'll use it once a week as a personal reminder that life is worth celebrating. If you stop by, I may let you use it as well.

# About the Author

Robert Tebo thought about writing a book for a very long time. Thinking and doing are two different things. Rather than write a book, he started a blog in the fall of 2017.

*Pondering Life's Lessons* is a compilation of several blogs written over the past five plus years. The first section focuses on his marriage to Ruth and the beginning of his family. The second includes his extended family and friends. The final section tells his story after Ruth's unexpected death.

He never anticipated writing the stories in the final section, but life doesn't go as we expect. We get what we get and learn to live through it as best we can.

We all have a story. We live it in bits and pieces each day. If we keep it to ourselves, it dies with us. Life's lessons are too important to let that happen. If his stories remind you of yours, please share them with those you love.

Bob's stories can be found at ihaveastoryforyou.net

www.ingramcontent.com/pod-product-compliance
Lightning Source LLC
Chambersburg PA
CBHW030149100526
44592CB00009B/197